SILENT VOICES

Monsoon Press

First Edition (English Language Version)

First published in the United Kingdom 2007

By Monsoon Press
In collaboration with Perfect Publishers

Silent Voices

All rights reserved. No part of this book may be reproduced may be adapted in any form known or to become know, now or at any time in the future, in any place be mechanical, electronic or other means of copying, printing, storage, retrieval, transmission, performance, broadcast, (whether terrestrial or extra terrestrial i.e. satellite) dramatic, literary, theatrical or musical production of any sort of whatsoever without the prior written permission of Monsoon Press Ltd or their duly authorised reprographic, performing, or other relevant rights organizations, or as expressly permitted by law.

The Moral rights of Monsoon Press have been asserted.

Printed in England by Lightning Source UK
Typeset in Adobe Caslon Pro by Bookcraft Ltd, Stroud, Gloucestershire

ISBN 978-0-9557267-0-5

Monsoon Press
Oxford House
2 Derbyshire Street
London
E2 6HG

Contents

Foreword	*Dr Martin Orwin*	v
Acknowledegements	*Rabina Khan*	vi
Zahrah Awaleh	*Daughter of Diaspora*	1
Shafi Said	*The Lost Pariah*	26
Adam Dirir	*We are Not Invisible*	64
Abdi Bahdon	*The Noble Savage*	73
Laila Ali Egge	*Letter to The Horn*	87

Foreword

The writing in this volume brings together five young people from the Somali community in the UK. We hear what they have to say, unmediated, about their concerns, joys, fears and hopes. This is a rare insight and is a valuable counter to what is often found in the mainstream media. Although the experience they write about is often shared by other Somalis, what we read here comes from individuals with distinct voices, and the passion with which they express themselves speaks to us directly because of this. For example the anger which shows itself in Zahrah Awaleh's writing on female genital mutilation is something that would not be found in an official report on this practice and this complements the way she shows it to be a practice not sanctioned by Islam. Through this piece we hear from an individual Somali woman which makes it all the more powerful and valuable. In the haunting story of Dwayne, Shafi Said treats violent Islamic militancy in a way which contrasts with the manner this is handled in newspapers and allows insight through the story that is lacking in other writing. We also learn from Shafi's imaginative writing what it is like to turn up at Boosaaso airport as a young Somali woman from the UK wearing jeans!

The writing here is very varied and reminds us how important it is to listen to what individual people have to say when the wider society has a more generalised or incomplete view of what it is to be Somali in the UK. Being Somali, and with that being Muslim, African and part of an immigrant community, is expressed here by young writers who I hope will continue to write and make their voices heard. Monsoon and Rabina Khan are to be congratulated for publishing this anthology, and I hope it gains the wide readership it deserves.

Dr Martin Orwin
London School of Oriental and African Studies

Acknowledgements

Rabina Khan

Silent Voices is the result of a project called Unearthing the Somali Voice part of Monsoon Press's Hidden Voices Programme funded by the Arts Council. The project enabled unknown Somali writers to contribute to an anthology that explores personal and poignant experiences through various forms of writing. For the writers and myself it was a creative journey into what could be achieved by working together. I was privileged to have found such wonderful and talented writers; Zahrah, Adam, Shafi, Abdi and Leila and with their enthusiasm and hard work Silent Voices was published.

    I would also like to thank the following people and organisations for their support and guidance Charles Beckett (Arts Council), Penguin, MBA Literary Agents, East Side Books, Shahida Rahman (Perfect Publishers), Dr Martin Orwin, Rageh Omaar, Fatima Begum, Christine Plumb, Monsoon Press Team, Somali Voice, and News International.

Daughter of Diaspora

Zahrah Awaleh

Zahrah Awaleh (1974-) was born in Scunthorpe, South Humberside, now located in North Lincolnshire, England. The town was a booming steel town when her father arrived and settled there in the 1950's. Consequently, her mother joined him there with the two eldest children in 1972. Shortly after her father's death in 1984, the family moved to Sheffield, South Yorkshire, where Zahrah completed her secondary education in 1990. In the same year, the family moved to London where she later read Arabic at the School of Oriental and African Studies (SOAS). She returned there to read a Masters in Islamic Studies after working in Hargeisa, Somaliland with the United Nations Population Fund (UNFPA). It was through the UNFPA and other UN agencies and NGOs in Hargeisa that Zahrah was exposed to campaigns against Female Genital Mutilation (FGM). This experience had a profound effect and lead to the writing of her Masters dissertation, which was based on the thesis that FGM is antithetical to Islam. Following her Masters, Zahrah went on to work with the London-based NGO Foundation for Women's Health, Research & Development (FORWARD), which runs national and international projects and campaigns against FGM and other forms of gender violence.

'Becoming a British Muslim' and 'Globe Souk' were originally written for the Art & Culture page, and the FGM article was originally written for the Family page for islamonline.net, and she currently writes for them.

Zahrah holds a Post Graduate Diploma and Qualification in Careers Guidance, and currently works as a Careers Adviser with Connexions in London. She is married with two children and lives in Ilford, Essex. If you would like to contact her via e-mail, her address is: z_awaleh@yahoo.com

Becoming A British Muslim

I find myself having to justify who I am now on a regular basis. I used to think it was quaint, but now it's just increasingly annoying. I am a Black British-born Muslim woman living in London. People have told me that I resemble someone Sudanese, Sri Lankan, Indian, Eritrean, and even Egyptian. I'm actually Somali, but Somali ethnicity, history, culture, and language contain threads of shared experience with the above peoples. This would add to the doubt surrounding the whole notion of exclusive "ethnicity" or "culture" in the field of social science, but that's another story.

My father arrived in the United Kingdom as a young man in the 1950s and quickly joined the booming steel industry of the then world-renowned British Steel Corporation. He married and eventually brought his young wife over with their two children from Northern Somalia in 1972 to settle in the steel town of Scunthorpe, South Humberside. I am the fourth child and the second to have been born here, and though the Somali community was tiny within Scunthorpe, I remember how close the families were to one another, how strong the friendships were among all the children. I also made good friends outside of the Somali community with children from diverse backgrounds, which included English, Bengali, Pakistani, and Jamaican. I left Scunthorpe when I was 1 years old, moving to Sheffield for four years, then to London in 1990 where I've lived ever since. I've always lived amongst the Somali community wherever I resided in the United Kingdom, while enjoying close and lasting friendships with people outside of it, and this is part of the blessing of living in probably the most multicultural society on the planet.

The two times I lived outside the United Kingdom, as a language student in Egypt and as a long lost daughter in Somaliland, I found myself struggling to adapt to both cultures, even though they are situated in countries that are predominately Muslim. While I was in Somaliland, I had to think deeply about my identity all the time because it was under so much scrutiny by almost everyone I met. They had not met many British-born Somali women that carried their dual heritage with pride, and who, by their description, practiced Islam with more conviction than they appeared to. Once I got back to the United Kingdom in 1998, I was thrilled to be back in my indigenous homeland, yet I still felt somewhat like a stranger.

I believe now that this was largely due to my understanding of Islam, which was still heavily influenced by a very narrow minded branch of the Salafi movement of my college and university days in the 1990s. Leaders of that movement constantly reminded us followers that the best of times for Muslims had come and gone with the Prophet (peace be upon him) and his Companions (may Allah be pleased with them all), and that all we could hope to achieve now was to remain "strangers" in this world (*dunya*), existing on the periphery and detached from the filth of mainstream modern society.

Since 9/11, Muslims in the West have experienced intense criticism like never before, and it made me reassess my Muslim identity and the Muslim community in Britain. Consequently, I have realised that Muslims individually and collectively are partly to blame for their marginalisation in British society because, in a lot of ways, that's where they think they belong. This is mainly due to their having an inferiority complex as immigrants and the other extreme of professing a superior tradition of morality within Islam, thus appearing to be extremely arrogant in the eyes of non-Muslims.

As I said previously, I was heavily influenced by the huge Islamic revivalist movement in the United Kingdom, in London especially, while I was an undergraduate at the School of Oriental and African Studies (SOAS), University of London, in the early to mid–1990s. I was a prominent member of the Islamic Society (ISOC) and we attempted to establish a small Muslim community at SOAS with quite good results. However, the bubble burst once everyone graduated because we had to enter the real world, gain employment, and work with non-Muslims. Something I suspect most of my peers in the ISOC were not used to at all. Our aims in the ISOC had been quite narrow; most important was the relearning of Islam via classical religious texts whose interpretation was strongly Hanbali or Salafi. The crucial matter that we didn't learn, however, was the modern comparative interpretation of those classical religious texts that allowed differences of opinion and diversity within Islam, along with adaptation according to time and place. This would definitely have made us more at ease with living Islam in Britain, while being confident Muslims and good, actively participating citizens. There were countless missed opportunities at university for many Muslims to participate in mainstream groups that concerned themselves with mainstream issues, such as student debt, human rights, the environment, and poverty. Had there been involvement in such groups, non-Muslims would have seen that Muslims generally could care for issues beyond their own "minority issues" and stand up for causes that had a greater impact on the wider society.

Post–9/11, Muslim groups and individuals have been working very hard to explain to British society that Islam is not a "religion of terrorism." Soon after the terrible event in New York, I felt the pressure from British society, especially the media, to assimilate or perish. This has made me realise that my origin is essentially British through and through. When I am asked where I come from now, instead of saying "Somalia," I say "Britain," not because I'm ashamed of my ethnic origin or embarrassed that someone might think I am a refugee. I am British, and a British Muslim first, because this is and always has been my home. English is my first language, though it isn't my mother's. I was educated here and this is where I feel I belong. I feel very passionately about establishing strong Muslim communities in Britain, and presently I work closely with a Somali refugee community group, helping members to integrate themselves and their families into British society. Similarly, I am very enthusiastic about getting involved in mainstream issues that may or may not directly benefit the Muslim community, but will definitely benefit the wider society: the anti-war movement and the green movement, for example.

The British Labour government claims to be in tune with the needs of the British Muslim community. On the one hand, it rushed the introduction of the Prevention of Terrorism Act 2005, which gives the Home Secretary the power to issue "control orders" to restrict the liberty of individuals without trial or appeal, enforcing them to stay under house arrest indefinitely. This is in contradiction to the European Human Rights Act that the Labour government proudly introduced in 1998; thus Labour had to withdraw certain clauses to pass the act. Then on the other hand, just last month on June 9, Labour introduced the Racial and Religious Hatred Bill 2005 into parliament. The bill is an extension of the original 1986 Public Order Act that prohibits incitement to racial hatred and which protected Sikhs and Jews (because the law said they were racial groups), but not Muslims (because they do not make up one racial group).

It is extremely ironic and disturbing that the Labour government has made every British Muslim a potential "terrorist" by the existence of the Prevention of Terrorism Act 2005, then tried to "alleviate" its negative impact on Muslims by speedily introducing the Racial and Religious Hatred Bill 2005. This merely helps to confuse the British public, who don't know whether they should fear Muslims (more than they used to) or not. The bill simply may not have been necessary had the act not existed and highlights yet again the hypocrisy and stealth tactics that Blair has become notorious for. Blair is determined to drag Britain kicking and screaming behind Bush's "War on Terror."

Thankfully, Muslims in Britain have started to wake up and get politically active by joining the anti-war movement, protesting against the many innocent victims of the anti-terror legislation, and switching from being staunch Labour supporters to voting for the Liberal Democrats and independent parties, such as Respect, in the May 2005 general elections.

Muslims have always contributed immensely to European history; thus Professor Tariq Ramadan suggests that the "duty of Muslims is to take Islam from the periphery of European culture to its centre"[1]. This would be achieved by Muslims becoming active citizens and adapting Islam to modern living while respecting its original intent. Muslims don't want to be "tolerated" by the British public because tolerance implies the majority has to suffer the presence of the "minority" if it so wishes. Muslims want to be accepted as equal citi-

---

1   *Emel Magazine*, May–June 2005

zens with equal opportunities and rights, as a community whose worldview and various cultures can contribute enormously to the diverse mosaic of traditions that constitute modern British culture and society.

    I have just come into work this morning and learned about several blasts going off in central London. There are injuries, but I still don't know if there have been any deaths. Obviously, I'm repulsed by such cowardly tactics as these, which have brought a cloud of gloom over London and the rest of the United Kingdom, places that had such an air of hope and excitement surrounding the peaceful protests over the G8 Summit, as well as yesterday's news of London winning the Olympics in 2012. The perpetrators of today's tragedy should be brought to justice; however I'm afraid that the anti-terror laws here will just impede that and destroy the lives of innocent people in the process.

The Gift – A Monologue

I have an appointment today to see a doctor at Guy's Hospital for an operation. Not no ordinary hospital operation. I was circumcised at the age of eight; well, actually, it wasn't a circumcision, because if it had been, there'd be no reason for me to see this doctor today. 'Circumcision' is the politically correct name for what happened to me. It even sounds acceptable, pleasing with its soft sibilants; clinically sound: 'circumcision with precision.' Bloodless, painless, unconscious even. An everyday affair. Numb. What about Female Genital Cutting, or FGC? More upfront, but still sterile and neat. It keeps those who practise it happy enough perhaps, as it's quite neutral, non-judgmental, I suppose.

On the other hand, Female Genital Mutilation, or FGM, is more blatant, offensive and even refreshing in some ways. Mutilation can be done with or without consent, but ultimately, in my opinion, mutilation sounds like it's done by force and with malice. Some mothers say they do it as an 'act of love.' Perhaps, that's what their mothers told them. Few 'acts of love' impose so much bloodletting, excruciating pain, and confusion upon a girl child who has no clue as to why her mother is killing her.

The only explanation being, "It's what we do, everyone does it, it's our culture." The girl becomes a woman and still doesn't understand why this happens and will one day have to choose whether or not to do it to her daughters. If not as an 'act of love,' then as an act of compliance to convention and religion, even though religion, at least Islam, makes little mention of it. So what? In this matter, religion serves an age-old tradition.

I don't know of any culture or community who practises Female Circumcision Proper, because what purpose could there be in cutting off the prepuce of the clitoris? I've heard that some Muslim Malaysians practise this because it *improves* the woman's sexual sensitivity, rather than abates it, as it is commonly understood to do. The most common form of FGM is the partial or total cutting of the clitoris, and that is no 'circumcision,' that is plain 'excision': that is mutilation.

The one part of the human body in either male or female ever created solely for pleasure is the most guilty.

That's why it's the most popular part to cut down and be rooted out. Why do these people think that they can take away what God Himself gave to each woman as a gift? A gift for all the crap that she has to put up with in life: from child molesters (usually found within the family), menstruation, men, to childbirth and losing her figure, to menopause, HRT, and losing her looks. What is the clitoris guilty of anyway? It's just a tiny bit of flesh made to give women sexual pleasure. Islam advocates that sex is *good* within marriage, even in the holy month of fasting! (i.e. Ramadan, and for your information check out the second chapter of the Koran). Furthermore, the Prophet Muhammad said that men should practice foreplay with their wives and not just mount them like beasts. Where did we go wrong?

Well, what I'm about to do today may be seen as sacrilegious by some members of my family or by those of my Somali community. On the whole, they practise FGM Type 3, as the WHO would say (so polite!?). This is when the vulva is closed by normally cutting off the clitoris, and gutting the inner or outer lips, only to stitch them together with sutures, thread, or even thorns.

The pitiful girl child is normally subjected to this torture with several kinswomen holding her down, since she has not been given any anaesthetic to relieve the horrific pain. If she's "lucky" enough to have a local or general anaesthetic, then she's numb to what's going on down there, so she doesn't feel the enormity of what she's losing. According to Somali tradition, a woman should wait to be "opened" until she's about to be married or even wait until the wedding night itself. In the old days, the husband would have to prove his virility, his 'manhood,' by opening it during his first penetration, which could take up to several weeks for him to get in completely. Imagine that?!

In recent years, a trend has come about where a Traditional Birth Attendant, a TBA, or nurse, comes along a few days before, or perhaps even on the wedding day itself, to open the vulva and instruct the patient on how to care for the wound. And as soon as that spot is opened, attempts at intercourse immediately follow.

So what are women meant to feel about sex in Somali culture? That it IT HURTS LIKE HELL! That's what. If it doesn't hurt physically due to the fact that what's left – a 'fake 2-in-1 vagina and piss hole' – is about the size of the average woman's fingertip, then what's happening on the emotional and psychological levels as he simply *approaches* her?

Perhaps her body trembles remembering how it was violated long ago in its most vulnerable place by the one who carried it and screamed bearing it. Or she closes her eyes and tries to hold back her tears and sobs, whilst her husband is blissfully unaware. Or it may mean pushing her partner off of her, yelling that she doesn't want sex that night. It may be the first time and he's got a blade ready; he'd rather cheat and take a short cut to getting in, risking his "manhood" coming under attack if anyone found out. All this so that she's in less pain, but then he might strike a main artery, especially critical around the clitoris which has so much blood connected to it, so there's a risk of haemorrhaging and even dying. So on seeing the blade she runs for her life into the toilet and locks herself in for the night.

After living with my scarred wound for so long and coming to terms with it by reading, debating, crying, sobbing and raging with God *(Why me?! Why didn't you stop them?)*, it took a period of depression for me to finally realise that the only way for me to resist this *shit* – no other word can do – and pull myself out was by taking serious action. No more talking. I began to see that the whole experience of FGM was a circle: the girl is viciously "closed" to preserve her virginity and shut out the demons or perverts that would certainly infiltrate her chastity *(For real! At least in my culture anyway!)*, and only be "opened" for the groom upon her marriage to him. Well, I've decided to break the circle. Now. Before I'm married. For me.

It's not for him, not for my parents, not for my so-called "culture." *What kind of culture does this to a human being anyway?!* It's for ME. It's a gift to myself: *I am my own gift to myself.* Somalis call a young unmarried woman *gashaanti*, meaning 'young virgin' in everyday terms. However, linguistically it means: 'she who is a gift for the household of her husband,' or 'she, the gift who enters the marital home of her husband.' It could also mean: 'the gift from which the husband derives sexual pleasure when he enters her.' Today is a gift to myself: *I am my own gift to myself.*

It has taken me months, no, *years*, to accept the fact that my body is my own property, and that I have every right to do this operation. I'm a Muslim woman and I don't want to transgress any laws of Islam, especially those relating to modesty. Yet I must do this one thing for myself, or I will lose my self-respect and even the will to live, and there's nothing in the laws of Islam that says what I'm about to do is a sin:

Today is a gift to myself: *I am my own gift to myself.*

Female Genital Mutilation and ISLAM

What does Islam say about FGM?

Female Genital Mutilation (FGM) is the partial or total elimination or changing of the external female genitalia, for cultural or non-therapeutic reasons.

Male circumcision is the cutting of the foreskin on the penis to enhance cleanliness (*taharah*). It is an established *Sunnah* (practice of Prophet Muhammad, peace be upon him). On the other hand, FGM is not a *Sunnah* nor is it equivalent to male circumcision, as we shall note later. Even, the mildest type (Type 1) normally involves cutting a part of or the whole of the clitoris: its skin and flesh. FGM has no therapeutic benefits, instead it has long-term and short-term health consequences that have damaged the lives of over 138 million women and girls in 28 countries in Africa, the Middle East, Asia, and increasingly among communities in the USA, Europe and Australasia.

FGM is a violation of the bodily integrity and dignity of women and girls and can have serious health consequences. In the short term, they can suffer violent pain, post-operative shock and clitoral haemorrhage. These last two outcomes could both lead to death. The long-term consequences include problems menstruating, urinary and kidney infections, sexual frigidity and psychological problems regarding body image.

FGM is prohibited in the UK by the 2003 FGM Act. Any UK national or permanent resident caught practising FGM in the UK or abroad, or anyone serving as an accomplice to it, is liable to be imprisoned for up to 14 years or fined – or both. This is irrespective of whether the country has laws against FGM or not. There are many African countries that have passed laws against FGM including: Kenya; CAR; Ghana; Togo; and Ivory Coast, among others. Thus, anyone who practises or aids someone in doing so in these countries could face imprisonment, fines or both.

The typical reasons given by *Sunni* Muslim practising communities (the majority of Muslims are *Sunni*) for doing FGM are:

protecting chastity/virginity; reducing sexual desire; and enhancing fertility and childbirth. However, FGM does not guarantee any of these. Rather, Type 3: closing over the urethral and vaginal openings with the gutted labia minora/majora and leaving a tiny hole that traps traces of urine and menstrual blood, could cause infections in the woman/child and complicate childbirth if the individual is not "opened" in time to avoid these.

No form of FGM has been proven to reduce sexual desire/promiscuity, however it may hinder sensitivity in sexual intercourse, thus having a devastating effect on women in later life when they marry/cohabit.

Promoting Chastity in Muslim Women

The Qur'an does not say that FGM is permissible, as many like to argue. Islam and the Qur'an don't hate women, rather men and women are said to originate from one soul (*Nafsun wahida*, Chapter 4, verse 1), making them equal before God. In addition, men are said to be the protectors (*Qawwamun*, Chapter 4, verse 34) of women, and God has ordered both men and women to be modest in their gaze and guard their chastity towards one another (Chapter 34, verses 30–31). There is no emphasis on women only. In fact, God ordered the men first to lower their gaze and guard their chastity! These verses confirm that FGM in Muslim communities is unnecessary, and it is God-consciousness (*taqwa*) that keeps a Muslim man and woman from illegal sexual intercourse/thoughts and not the absence of any part of their genitalia. *FGM is no guarantee against illegal sexual intercourse, be it pre-marital or extra-marital.*

The Islamic Right to Sexual Fulfilment in Marriage

In Chapter 30, verse 21 of the Qur'an, it says:

> And among His signs is this, that He created for you mates from among yourselves, that ye may dwell in tranquillity with them, and He has put love and mercy between your (hearts); Verily in that are signs for those who reflect.

The above verse describes the ideal marital relationship for Muslims, and it is the right of every Muslim to find a mate and achieve all the benefits that necessarily come with that. FGM, however, does not allow a woman to enjoy sexual intercourse fully because of:

1. The lack of sensation she may experience due to not having a full and healthy clitoris and other external genitalia;
2. Flashbacks of the FGM operation on her wedding night;
3. Problems relating to the infibulation when, in many cases, the husband has to "open" her using forcible penetration (or even an object) on the wedding night and thereafter until he can penetrate her easily and leave a permanent hole for himself;
4. She may experience other problems trying to sexually relate to her husband because of the negative attitude towards her sexuality;
5. Not understanding her Islamic right to sexual enjoyment as well.

Dr Jamal Badawi speaks out against FGM/FC

The well-known Canadian-Egyptian Islamic scholar, Dr Jamal Badawi, uses the term 'Female Circumcision' in his work 'Gender Equity in Islam, Appendix: Is Female Circumcision Required' (1995)[2] to refer to the following:

1. Type I: Removal of the hood (prepuce) of the clitoris only;
2. Type II: Removal of the entire clitoris (cliterodectomy) along with part of the labia minora, which is sutured together, leaving an opening;
3. Type III: Removal of the entire clitoris, labia minora and medial part of the labia majora, stitching both sides of the vulva together, leaving a small opening. This is known as the 'Pharaonic procedure.'

Dr Badawi clearly states that 'the second and third procedures were never mandated, encouraged or even consented to by the Prophet (pbuh).' Furthermore he condemns Types II and III as

---

2 http:www.jannah.org/genderequity/equityappendix.html

MUTILATION and says 'nothing justifies genital mutilation. In fact, no mutilation is allowed by Islam even in the battlefield. Not only are these two procedures unjustifiable, they are brutal, inhumane and in violation of Islam.'

Dr Badawi continues, that FC is not in the Qur'an and no *hadith* (saying of the Prophet (pbuh)) requires it, but some appear to accept it: For example, "Circumcision is a commendable act for men (*Sunnah*) and is an honourable thing for women (*Makromah*)."[3]

Badawi explains the *hadith*, saying that '*Makromah*' has no religious obligation, and that the *hadith* is weak according to scholars of *hadith*, so it is unreliable to justify the act of FC.

Dr Badawi quotes the next *hadith* as being more authentic, and it is reported by Umm Atiyyah: "Cut off only the foreskin (outer fold of skin over the clitoris; the prepuce) but do not cut off deeply (i.e. the clitoris itself), for this is brighter for the face (of the girl) and more favourable with the husband."[4]

If cutting the prepuce of the clitoris is allowed in Islam, according to the above hadith, then, Dr Badawi concludes, it is meant to enhance sexual pleasure, not curtail it! This is clear from the wording, "for this is brighter for the face (of the girl) and more favourable with the husband," meaning she will still derive physical pleasure from the intimacy and that will please her husband and consequently heighten his sexual satisfaction as well. Therefore, FC in this case stands in direct contradiction to the arguments for it by its proponents, as it does not control by reducing female sexual appetites – rather it increases them! In addition, there is no 'selective curtailment' in the Qur'an or *Sunnah* that restricts the sexual activities of one gender as this is blatantly biased. Badawi goes on, 'Furthermore, chastity and virtue are not contingent on "cutting off" part of any sensitive and crucial human organ. Rather, they are contingent on spiritual and

---

3 Al-Shawkani, *Nayl Al-Awtar*, Dar Al-Jeel, Beirut, 1973, Vol. 1, p. 139

4 Al-Tabarani, quoted in Al-Albani, Muhammad N., *Silsilat Al-Ahadeeth al-Sahiihah*, Al-Maktab al-Islami, Beirut, Lebanon, 1983, Vol. 2, Hadeeth no. 722, pp. 353–358 especially pp. 356–357.

moral values (his bold) of the person and the supporting virtuous environments.'

For those who argue that Type I is '*Sunnah*,' Dr Badawi argues that the Prophet (pbuh) only used '*Sunnah*' whilst referring to male circumcision, not FC, so it is not religiously obligated. Dr Badawi quotes some (like the late Rector of Al-Azhar University, Shaykh Gad Al-Haque) who advocate that Type I is permissible, since the Prophet (pbuh) did not ban it, and no total ban can be placed upon it. However, he proposes, 'it is within the spirit of *Shariah* (Islamic Law) to restrict something that is permissible if discovered to be harmful.' Thus, Type I FC could be banned (the other two by their very nature are prohibited as previously noted) based upon the well-known *Shariah* principle of *Al-Dharar Yozul* (harm must be removed). Type I is not as radically painful as Types II and III. Nevertheless, Dr Badawi says it can be argued to be 'painful, traumatic and often performed in an unhygienic setting leading to infection and other problems.' Furthermore, even if a physician were to do the procedure, the prepuce of the clitoris is so delicate and tiny (much tinier in small girls) that very few could confess to executing the procedure properly.

In addition to Dr Badawi's comments above, *Al-Masalih al-Mursala* ('the public welfare') is a principle in Islamic jurisprudence that is used by all *Sunni* schools. It advocates the general principle of 'no hardship' and a sub-clause to it is known as *Sadd al-Dhara'i'* ('blocking the ways to evil'), which involves preventing the spread of evil practices; even if they are *halal* in theory, they become *haram* due to their dangerous consequences. All Types of FGM/FC certainly fall within this category, whichever *Sunni* school of thought one looks at, due to its pernicious effects in any society, therefore making it prohibited under Islamic law (see for example, 'The Lawful and the Prohibited in Islam' by Dr Yusuf Al-Qardawi for details).

Conclusion

In conclusion, the Qur'an states in Chapter 2, verse 185:

> God intends every facility for you; He does not want to put you to difficulties.

Islam came to bring glad tidings, not bad news, and enlighten the ignorant, not keep them in darkness. Thus, the Qur'an confirms once again that Islam and FGM are totally incompatible.

Islam does not allow its followers to harm themselves intentionally, and it vehemently protects the rights of women and children, who are amongst the weakest of groups in every society.

The Prophet Muhammed (pbuh) said in a *hadeeth* on treating women well, reported by Abu Hurayrah (may Allah be pleased with him): 'The believers with the most complete *iman* (faith) are those with the most refined manners. And the best among you are those who are best to their women.' (recorded by At-Tirmithi and Ibn Hibban).

We can conclude from our analysis that all forms of FGM/FC are not Islamic; rather they are harmful and require a total ban in order to safeguard the health and well being of Muslim women throughout the Muslim world for all time.

The Globe Souk

As I entered the Globe *Souk*, a replica of a traditional Arabian market, the absolute noise was the first thing that hit me. I was overwhelmed by this frenzy of activity located in the basement hall of the Globe Exhibition Center in London. Natural light was lacking. In its place, the low orchestrated artificial lighting brought about an evening atmosphere, almost twisting one's concept of time. One could easily lose oneself here. So much was happening in such a small space, yet everything was organised, perfectly proportioned, like a chocolate box – all I had to do was choose the first tantalising morsel.

The *Souk* was packed with visitors, stalls, a Peter Saunders exhibition, a gallery of exhibits from The Prince's School of Traditional Arts, and a café. I didn't know where to start in this cave-like dream of a *souk*. However, my son's irritation informed me that I'd better feed him his lunch first before embarking on my whirlwind tour. So, when I saw the Qur'an reciter's Moroccan seat was vacant, I promptly sat myself down to feed my son his lunch of miniature cheese sandwiches. This was to the surprise and delight of passers-by, who may have thought me slightly audacious, or may have envied me for getting there first!

With baby fed and reunited with his father and elder sister, I was left to briefly indulge myself in The Globe *Souk* experience. On offer were lush dark blue and green glass hookahs (tall water pipes to burn fruit-flavored tobacco), for those who wanted to rekindle memories of smoking them in an old café in Cairo, Tunis, or Fez. There were the ubiquitous frames filled with modern and traditionally styled Arabic calligraphy, as well as Moroccan lanterns and lamps, lit up to add to the authentic atmosphere. In front of the stage was a wide selection of delicious Lebanese sweets and savories, which I was fortunate enough to sample. I must say, the rose water in the sweets was extremely fragrant, making them highly delectable. Opposite was the Palestinian General Delegation's sea of blue Palestinian ceramic ware, and wooden pieces that included a chess set and a model of the holy city of Jerusalem.

I managed to escape into the gallery of traditional art exhibits for a few moments. The tent canopy over it kept out most of the sound, making it an oasis of peace surrounded by the cacophony of voices and perpetual movement. The pieces consisted of mainly geometric shapes created in mediums of ceramic, paint, and wood, which were framed and hung. There were pictures of a Jesus figure, and elsewhere a calligraphy piece of *Allahu Ahad* (Allah is One), painted white on a black background. The other exhibits were just as eclectic. I even viewed a selection of poems dedicated to various religious subjects, written in old English script and with miniature watercolor pictures set beside the verses.

Rezia Wahid creates exquisitely fine hand-woven textiles using a contemporary loom. Her loom reminded me of antique looms, and I was sure it would have felt at home in a museum. Rezia was, nevertheless, very proud of her elegant workhorse and, more importantly, of the beautiful results – fine pure silks and mixed silk and Egyptian cotton, hand-woven textiles for clothing or frames. One piece with a blue border was an homage to the famous Turkish blue found mostly in *Iznik* ceramics, which were also on offer in the *Souk*.

As I was chatting to someone I hadn't seen for years, a man in front of me dressed in a *thawb* (Arab men's long garment) shouted, "Stop thief!" I nearly jumped out of my skin. I thought there had been a genuine mugging, but it turned out to be a lively start to another of the Khayaal Theatre Group's *Souk Stories*, on show at the stage besides the stalls. Phew!

Clive Rogers deals in oriental rugs from Central Asia and the Near East. He also sells embroideries, shawls, pictures, and furniture from the two regions. He had a particularly elegant pine and cedar chair from Damascus with exquisite mother of pearl inlay that is circa 1890.

I also got chatting to Farrah Irfan, who is the director of her own clothing company for Pakistani women. She specialises in silk and chiffon outfits, handmade embroideries and shawls, and Afghani handicrafts.

The ringing of a bell breaks up the continuous hustle and bustle to announce the next show of *Souk Stories*, and some people start to head for the stage. I head for the Peter Saunders exhibition, but I end up detouring to a stall with Chinese-Arabic calligraphy by the hand of one Haji Noor Deen. He is a Chinese Muslim who has a unique style of combining Chinese script with Arabic in various ways on paper scrolls. I observed an astonishing piece that read "I love Muhammad" in Chinese, but that contained the Shahadah (the Muslim Testimony of Faith) inside it in a tiny feathery Chinese-like Arabic script, which seems to be his signature style. At the top was written: *Bismillah Ar-Rahman Ar-Rahim*, which is Arabic for "In the Name of Allah, The Most Gracious, The Most Merciful," in a geometric style, but not Arabic; he explained that it was more Chinese than Arabic. Another piece was the more familiar rendition of the ninety-nine names of Allah in Arabic, with a hadith below it: "It is reported by Abu Hurayrah that whoever memorises the ninety-nine Names of Allah will enter Paradise."

Before I could discuss anything else with Haji Noor Deen, I had to leave, as the *Souk* was closing. On the stage, there was an auction of the stage props and the seat that I had previously rested upon. The crowd was getting excited and going nowhere. So much for home time!

The Mother

We bear the burden
For nine months, more or less:
Nausea
Dizziness
Vomiting
Thirst
Quick hunger
Stretches
Heaviness
Tightness

The body expands to allow space, then more space
Till there is no more
And the burden has to be born

So the body knows what to do
Like many mothers before
It squeezes almost the life out of itself
To bear another
Out of generosity
And with no thought for itself

No voice for the excruciating pain
Just moan after moan
No energy for anything else
Except pushing, only at the end

The body bears each contraction with sublime grace
Only the *nafs* screams with pain
Wondering when the torture will end
Desiring to put a rest to it all
And just depart this life right now;
If only

No sweeter relief can a soul taste
When the burden is finally, mercifully born
No care for cuts, bruises and tears
The body has released the other;
The child

Both are at last free of each other
Only to be reunited;
Tired and wounded,
To lie down to sleep together
And bask in the silence of victory and love

Prayer

I bowed down
He heard my prayer
Made my heart
Sound
Better
Whole
Nourished
Sharper
Lighter
Luminescent
Ready to carry my load
With bright eyes

The Lovers

Two lovers met on the path
And chose the other's company
For the journey to the Beloved
Their destiny becoming one
Entwined henceforth
Their hearts
Turned to one another
By none other
Than the Keeper of Hearts
So fragile the bond
Yet so enduring along the journey
It bewilders the lovers
This "love"
The heart soars to the heavens
Riding upon wings of heady delight
Only to fall
To fly once more
And suffer the depths of agony
To taste exquisite ecstasy
Of union with the beloved
And the final reunion with the Source of love: *Al-Wadud*

On my way home

I noticed a cloud today
On my way home
And I suddenly remembered where I was:
For a moment I was in awe,
Silenced by the sheer majesty of it all.
I smiled to myself:
I had come home.

A typical day

A typical day
And night
Is there day and night
Or just a stream of time?
Does it matter?

Everything is a blur
Of nappies
Milk
Breastfeeding
Meal times and snacks
Leaving me spinning
My head aching
My back nearly buckling
Under the duress
Of carrying my load

But in the midst of all this
Are glimpses of sanity and tranquillity
That remind me of the value
Of having a family

What of love?

What of love?
So many shapes and sizes
Take what fits best
Nearest
Then make it your own
Or never taste it
Feel it
Ever

Waiting for that nourishing love
That staple diet of a love
So elusive, so fragile
Wanting it too much can break your heart
Bring fierce pangs of hunger
Yet no one fasts forever
But once the fast is over
The hunger's gone
You remember what you dreamt of
What you never even knew you dreamt of
Just felt beneath the surface
It rises up from time to time
Gushes
Leaving tracks of tears
And yearning
So much
You may die

What of love?
Why so hidden, so elusive
O Keeper of Hearts?
So I seek You more feverishly
Here
To find You waiting for me

There
Enveloping me
My mantle on the road
Finally entering into Your Warm embrace
Upon arrival?
If only
Then the weary journey
Of this weary traveller
As a way to You
Becomes the riding beast I call my friend

Awakening

I thought I was awake
Yet I was sleeping
Unaware of myself
My real person
Ever so quietly asleep
Perhaps I dreaded the world
And the burden of it all
Subconsciously
Ever so quietly
Unaware of myself

Till something inside unfurled
A beautiful dazzling light
Broke through
Beaming right through every pore
Illuminating all of my being
Like a closed flower
Dormant
Waiting
To one day blossom
Give light and fragrance
To all who sought it
Who too yearned for their awakening

The Lost Pariah ...

Shafi Said

Shafi Said was born on June 10, 1983 in Somalia to a nomadic family. One day while tending to his father's herd at a very young age, his aunt (may she rest in peace. See poem – 'tribute to my aunt') decided to take him to the city to gain some education and that is where his love for books started. But it wasn't long before the civil war broke out, extinguishing his dreams of education before they even began. In the years that followed, he stayed with his cousins with whom he later moved to the UK. On arriving in the UK, he enrolled in college and started working extensively with several Somali communities, many of which he still works with.

After completing a year studying Computer Systems Engineering at the University of Westminster, he decided to change courses and study something he enjoyed – writing. So he enrolled at the University of East London and is currently in his final year, working toward a combined honours degree in Journalism with Creative and Professional Writing.

Shafi now works as a Teaching Assistant at a school where he is also a School Governor. And along with fellow students from the university, he runs Exposed East, an online creative writing magazine that showcases student work. He also works on the magazine with Somali Eye Media.

Shafi is also currently working on his first book. He can be reached at: Shafisaid@googlemail.com. Or go to his weblog, http://shafisaid. wordpress.com, where he regularly writes about his experiences, cultural heritage and travels.

The Lost Pariah ...

It was a dark December night and the clocks were striking eleven. Darkness engulfed the narrow Oldman Street, and the few lampposts that dimly flickered in the distance became moth sanctuaries. In one of the houses, a light was lit and an old lady sat on a large creamy sofa facing the window. On her lap lay a child whom she observed with earnest eyes. She repeatedly stroked his golden hair, tenderly running her hand through every strand. As he passed by the window, Dwayne stood there for a while, and wondered what it felt like to be in that warm lap and to be so gently stroked.

He dragged his feet from the scene and continued on his walk. A few doors down Oldman Street was his home ... or where he lived. He didn't like to call it home for it did not seem like a home to him. As he approached the door, he looked up to see that the light in one of the upper rooms was lit. It was his Aunt Rochelle's room. Bracing himself for a harsh night, he traced the doorbell and pressed it once.

A few moments later, he heard someone descending the flight of stairs. His aunt opened the door and stood there staring at him.

"And what time do you call this?" she barked angrily, her eyes fixated on him.

Dwayne didn't say a word; he couldn't. Her big bulgy eyes glared with rage in the dark and her silhouette became magnified by the light from the stairway.

"I said what time do you call this? Do you think you can run aroun' all day n' expect to come n' sleep in *my* house?"

Again he didn't answer. She didn't expect an answer anyway.

It was freezing outside and all Dwayne ever wanted was to get inside the house, then she could scold him as long as she wanted. She enjoyed having such power over him and she made it no secret either.

"You wanna live in this house, you do as I say, you hear!" she'd snap, if Dwayne ever challenged her authority.

She continued shouting at him without regard for the sleeping neighbours. He was getting used to her insults and taunts for he heard them almost everyday. Unlike other kids of his age, he wasn't allowed to commit mistakes. A simple mistake of playing outside at times cost him dearly. However, the biggest mistake that he committed, in her eyes, was being Latoya's son.

Rochelle's elder sister, Latoya, had an acute brain injury from a severe car accident shortly after Dwayne was born thirteen years ago. Dwayne's father, Mark, died in the accident, and though Latoya survived, the psychological disturbance rendered her ineffective in carrying out her duties as a mother and looking after her son. She lost most of her memory and at times would narrate fictitious accounts of past events, believing them to be true and accurate. "My son was the bravest soldier in the World War. I remember it very well when he … " she'd start and relate a longwinded tale. After a few days she didn't remember having a son and strongly objected to it when told so.

Rochelle wasn't very fond of her elder sister, partly because she hated her husband who did not treat her well, and partly because she regarded her docile for allowing herself to be treated that way. With the health of her sister deteriorating, Rochelle was beholden to care for her nephew but with the strong hate for his father, it was difficult. From a very young age, she commanded him to clean the house, run errands and attend to all the household chores. Her unrelenting attitude towards him engendered a feeling of hatred that indignantly burned his insides. However, he had no choice but to stay with her, for he had no relatives or friends that were willing to take him in.

"You've got his devious eyes. You look *just* like your father," she would claim every time she saw him.

The time Dwayne spent standing outside the door while his aunt scolded him seemed like an eternity. Finally, she let him inside and slammed the door behind him. He went upstairs and into his room. He could not feel his hands and his toes. They had swollen up and gone numb due to the cold. The severity of his aunt's detestation towards him had broken his spirit. He was on the verge of bursting in anger and lashing out at her, but he respected her regardless of her ill will. He silently lay on his bed, tucked under his duvet, and listened to the howling of the wind for some comfort. Even though he wasn't crying, tears ran down his cheeks and, successively, tiny droplets slid down onto the pillow, until the shutters of his eyes slowly came together.

The morning broke, misty and wet, and a few deflected rays of sunshine penetrated the large windowpane and crept into the lavishly furnished living room. Dwayne had woken up earlier than usual and was passing along the corridor towards the toilet when he heard muffled noises coming from the living room. He stepped closer to the door and placed his ear against it.

"I don't want him in this house any more. I can't afford it any longer. I want him out, and I want him out now!" Dwayne heard Anthony yell at his wife.

"But where would he go if we let him out?" Rochelle replied.

"I couldn't care less!"

Afraid that they might come out any minute, he quickly ran to his room and closed the door behind him.

It was about half an hour later when Rochelle had started to get ready for work. She woke up her two children to get them ready for school, but not Dwayne. He never attended school; she didn't allow him. However, Dwayne was expected to wake up every morning and prepare breakfast for the children. Noticing that he hadn't woken up yet, his aunt shouted at the top of her voice.

"Wake up, you filthy piece of shit!"

There was no reply. She shouted again, this time, as she rarely does, calling him by his name. Again there was no reply.

"The little bastard is ignoring me!" she murmured in her teeth, walking toward his room to punch his lights out. With force, she pushed the door open and found herself standing in the middle of a tiny and dull attic. It was as neat and clean as it could have been and a beam of light luminously shone through a small window above the bed. She stood at the entrance, aghast, and examined the entire room for anywhere he could have hidden. She lifted up the valances and checked under the bed, but to no avail. As she turned to leave, she saw a piece of paper on top of the bed:

Goodbye.

Dwayne

Dwayne left the house and sauntered along the road with one aim – to get as far as possible away from his aunt. His breath came in heavy pants of cold air, which came out of his nostrils as smoke. His head spiralled out of control with lingering doubts and uncertainties. But amid the cold and confusion, a reassuring thought in the back of his head spelled out the word: *freedom.* On the other hand, a twinge of fear lay adamant among the newly-found freedom and managed to threaten him persistently.

By noon, Dwayne had covered about ten miles of land and, with a few more, ended up in the historical parts of Greenwich. Walking past the university and the central market, he headed straight for the Thames River. It was late afternoon, and whatever was left of the sun had started to plummet down the horizon, leaving behind trails of magnificent colours. The sky looked like an artist's flamboyant display of watercolours. The setting sun had left behind its imprints – a layer of orange formed an undercoat for a spellbinding image composed of several other layers of clouds, ranging from dark grey to lighter shades of red, dancing across the sky majestically. Standing at the banks of the Thames, Dwayne gazed at the horizon with admiration and his worries started to lessen. He watched as an aeroplane swam effortlessly through the clouds, disappearing in the thicker, darker grey clouds one moment, then reappearing in the lighter shades, leaving behind a blazing trail of bright orange.

The serene water reflected the bright conspicuous clouds and enclosed him in a cloak of tranquillity. There wasn't a tide or any disturbance, but a gentle breeze caressed the surface of the water, giving it a ripple effect. He stood there until the last few rays of the sun had plunged deeper and deeper into the horizon and darkness stealthily enveloped him. Even the people striding along the promenade had retreated to the warmth of their homes and the burning logs of their fires. This thought, combined with the darkness, caused the tense fear to return as he sat on the flight of steps by the Cutty Sark. It was in that moment that he realised that he was alone. He conjured up images of his small but cosy attic. At least there, he had a roof over his head.

His throat thickened with anger. He wanted to do something, scream, shout or even break something, but he resisted the urge and unzipped a backpack that he brought along with him. He took out a towel, spread it in a dark corner of a passage by the Thames, and curled up on it. With a few sheets covering him, he hugged his knees and placed his hands between them. He shivered a little, tightening his jaw to keep his teeth from clicking.

He cleared his mind and entered another realm, when distant noises caught his attention. It was late at night and unlikely for anyone to be around at such times. The noises came closer and closer until he could clearly hear them. He made out three distinct voices coupled by a few others.

"Should we jack 'im?" said one of them in a hoarse voice.

"Nah, allow it, man. It's cold, let's go!" said another in a lively voice. Dwayne took it that he was younger than the other.

A few others interrupted by talking at once, arguing whether to rob Dwayne of his only possession or to go about their way.

"Fuck it; we made our money tonight. Let's go," said a slightly older person in a stern voice.

The loud voices diminished to a murmur, as the sounds of footsteps faded with the distance.

Night after night, Dwayne heard them walk past him, shouting, arguing and fighting. One night, as Dwayne sat on his towel ready to sleep at his usual time, the group came by. They had come earlier than usual, and Dwayne was sure he would be hassled. They approached him, striding confidently, wearing multiple sweaters, one on top of the other, hoods obscuring their faces.

"Oi, wha' u doin' here?" enquired the first of the bunch who came close to him.

He didn't answer, but looked up at him to see if he could get a glimpse of his face.

Soon the others joined him and intently stared at him, as if unable to understand his sleeping rough.

"How old are you?" came a voice from his left.

Dwayne immediately recognised it as the stern voice that he heard a few nights before. He strained to see in the dark, his eyes blurring as he looked in the direction the voice came from.

"Thirteen," he softly replied.

"Fuck!" screamed the one at the front, standing at the brim of Dwayne's towel-marked territory. "And what da fuck are you doin' 'ere?"

They started muttering all together.

"Shut the fuck up!" said the guy with the stern voice.

There was silence all at once. Dwayne understood it that he was the one in charge. With his finger, he beckoned them to move away, which they did immediately, and he kneeled down beside Dwayne. Taking his hood off to reveal his dark face, he spoke calmly, setting Dwayne at ease and prompting him to reveal his reasons for being where he was. The guy introduced himself as James and offered to give Dwayne a place to stay.

"You want somewhere to stay?" he asked.

Dwayne dreaded the company of these nocturnal wanderers and whatever they were up to, but for a warm place to stay he was inclined to follow them. Besides, he didn't find the calm tone of James, and his self-possessed disposition, objectionable.

He packed his bag, stood up firmly, broadened his shoulders and, along with the group, disappeared into darkness.

There was complete silence among the group as they walked, and none dared question James as to why he had brought Dwayne along, even though some seemed to pity the boy with their welcoming glance. One of them even offered to carry his rucksack for him while another patted him on the shoulder compassionately. He wondered what he had gotten himself into, and their dubious fondness towards him, accompanied by their over eagerness, made him a little suspicious. They led him through a maze of streets, many twists and turns, dark alleys and abandoned garages, and then finally onto a dimly lit street. They marched with one single pace and Dwayne was finding it hard to keep up. Observing his surroundings, just in case anything happened, he noticed a signboard – "Steephill Road". The name in fact described the street, which was somewhat steep, the houses on it descending down the hill. Further down, at the bottom of the street was a block of shabby flats. The boys made their way straight into one of the blocks. Graffiti was painted on every reachable wall of the flat. Some were names, some insults, and on a corner, in enormous writing, was the word "Peckham". He made a mental note of that and went into the flat, up a series of stairs that reeked of urine and vomit, through some claustrophobic corridors, then into a wooden door at the end. Dwayne memorised the house number – 56 – and went in.

Contrary to the condition of the flat on the outside, the insides of their rooms were immaculate, with expensive furnishing. They went into a spacious living room, where an extraordinarily large Plasma Screen Television was mounted on the wall adjacent to a portrait of a pleasant-faced black man with dreadlocks. Beneath it, an ornamental desk accommodated a bulky Hi-Fi system and some trophies. A set of huge brown leather sofas took up the majority of the room. Positioned in the middle of the wooden-floored room was a square glass table that sat on a costly rug. Dwayne started to feel the warmness of the house and relaxed a little when he noticed the boys huddled up by a shiny silver chest in a corner. Upon opening it they waited for James to empty the contents, which he promptly did. He took out four large bags of money, bundles of twenty-pound notes, and laid them on the glass table. He put his hand in the chest once again and with it came out another three bags of what looked like powder, and another bag of dried, crushed leaves. Dwayne was perplexed, his mind tried to invent all sorts of justifications to make sense of what he had just seen, but to no avail.

Despite the effusive welcome given to Dwayne by the boys – The Peckham Boys, as he later learnt – and the inviting and cosy residence, something strongly troubled him inside. "What are you doing here, Dwayne?" an irritating voice in his head demanded to know, disrupting his moments of peace as he lay in his warm bed that night, enjoying the serenity of the bright moon that dazzled in the midst of the dark sky. "YOU SHOULDN'T BE HERE!" it shouted in his mind, but he managed to subdue it, calmly staring into the depths of the vast sky, which seemed enormous in the dark. The longer he stared into the gloom, the darker it became and the deeper it appeared – so deep and vast that its extent was unimaginable: invisible. However, in that immeasurably infinite labyrinth of dark space was a beautiful crescent, with a brightness that transcended anything on earth. Dwayne admired the moon, and his eyes lingered there as minutes rolled by. It was the first time he had seen the moon with a spirit of profound seriousness and sincerity. He was almost lost in a deep trance, with the moon indicative of forgotten pleasures and forbidden desires, when that nagging voice once again, like a pinprick, stabbed his conscious. Even in the vast darkness he thought he saw the figure of a man wildly gesticulating and shouting "NO!" at him, but he fought with himself to keep that voice at bay and not listen to it. However, time after time it would resurface and annoy him when he was most contemplative. With great difficulty, he managed to put his mind at ease, still enthralled by the moon, and steadily the darkness engulfed him as his eyes could see no more and his mind could wander no more.

It was the following afternoon when Dwayne woke up, surprising even himself. He hadn't slept so peacefully for as long as he remembered. The boys were good to him and didn't wake him up or disturb his sleep. It wasn't as if he was a guest of the house, but more of a member. And that worried him, but for reasons he didn't know. From that afternoon on, he followed the boys wherever they went. They didn't object to his presence, but they rarely ever involved him in their covert operations of the night; some even took place during the day at times. He had now become another member of the clique – an incompatible member.

Dwayne had, until now, led a simple life without self-indulgence and extravagance, for his possessions were limited in number and, in his impoverished existence, his wealth didn't allow room for any luxury. The boys, on the other hand, were extravagant in every sense of the word. From the lavish furnishings in the house to the designer clothes they wore to the cars they drove, theirs was a world dissimilar to what Dwayne was used to. Despite this, he tried to blend in and feel like his colleagues, wearing fashionable clothes every evening when the boys made their rounds.

On these trips, backwards and forwards, to places unfamiliar to him, Dwayne observed his surroundings as he always did. Every evening, as they walked past the riverbank, they came across a man sitting on a wooden bench, one leg on top of the other, his wooden walking stick by his side. Every time Dwayne saw him, the man's hollow black eyes seemed to pierce him, invoking in him a curiosity of a peculiar kind. Something in the man's eyes pulled him, but he couldn't figure out what it was. It was like the pleading stare a patient gives his nurse – insistent yet sympathetic. Even when he disappeared into the rusty and ravaged streets of Deptford and Peckham, the old man's gaze still gripped him like a magnet. There was something strange about that man that haunted Dwayne; something puzzling and inexplicable that made him eager to talk to him. An air of mystery surrounded the man like a thick fog and Dwayne wanted to find out what it was.

On one bright Sunday afternoon, when the boys were resting, Dwayne decided to go to the riverbank, this time alone, to see if the man was still there. Regardless of the brightness of the afternoon, the chilly December winds were still formidable and Dwayne's teeth began to click. He tightened his coat and kept walking. When he reached the riverbank, the old man was, as he anticipated, there. Dwayne walked in a casual, effortless way, on a flimsy pretext of enjoying his surroundings, looking over to the river at times, and from the corner of his eye, observing the old man. After some time of displaying such behaviour, he came and sat at the other end of the bench, where the old man was sitting, and gazed into the horizon. The old man was, as usual, in a reflective mood, his arms crossed as he stared into the river. No one said a word, though Dwayne was on the verge of letting his feelings out. He resisted. A long time had passed, and although the riverbank was noisy with activity, the silence was deafening and the wait for someone to break it insufferable. It was almost an hour later when Dwayne was rewarded for his patience.

"They are a very unscrupulous bunch. I'd be very careful if I were you, young man," said the old man in a strict manner.

Dwayne's eyes lit up with enthusiasm, not because of what was said by the man but because he finally spoke to him.

"Why do you say that?" Dwayne asked, reverting to the statement of the old man.

Another few moments of silence passed.

"Do you know them?" the old man replied, answering Dwayne's question with a question.

"Yes I do," replied Dwayne.

"How well?"

"Why do you care anyway?"

Dwayne was getting agitated. His eyes fiercely fixated themselves on the old man. He realised that since meeting his new friends, even trivial things became of much annoyance to him. Now the old man's questions annoyed him.

"Do you know what perception is, son?" asked the old man in a composed tone.

"No, why?" shot back Dwayne.

"It is how you see the world. It's the ability to discern your surrounding environment."

Dwayne was lost. What does perception or how he sees the world have to do with his friends? Or was the old age getting to him?

"What is your name, son?" asked the old man after a brief silence.

"Dwayne."

"You can call me Arthur."

Dwayne nodded.

"How do you see your world, Dwayne?"

"Like I'm stuck in a claustrophobic lift, with no way out."

Dwayne had not planned to give such a reply, but it came out spontaneously. For a moment, he wondered where it came from and what basis it had, but that was unfathomable.

"That's not how you see it, son. It's how you chose to see it. You can never see things the way they are until and unless you are willing and prepared to see them. Everything is based on perception; do not let ignorance cloud your perception. A thick cloud of darkness faces you now, hindering you from seeing past it. What you need to do is look deep into your soul and see what lies beneath the surface of you."

This forced Dwayne to contemplate for a while – contemplate upon the meaning of what the old man had just said.

"Stand up, Dwayne, and stand there!" said the old man, pointing to the pavement about two meters away from him. "Now tell me, what do you see?"

Dwayne did as he was told and looked at the old man. He thought it was a weird request but he did it anyway. He observed the old man's features – his grey hair, his wrinkly face, his moustache from which a few whiskers protruded untidily from the tip of his upper lip, his huge glasses that he held in his hands, his outdated clothing style – and related it all to him.

"By all means, you are right, for that *is* what you see; it's what you are *prepared* to see. You can say it's a description of me, but not your perception of me. Your perception of me would be what you *think* of me, rather than what you are willing to see. Do you follow me, son?"

Dwayne was slightly perplexed, but he was also beginning to grasp the concept of the old man. The man, whose eyes had such an alarming power that dismantled Dwayne's senses, and whom he was starting to admire, had lived to a ripe old age. His clothes, though plain and unfashionable in style, were immaculate and neatly pressed. A long, grey overcoat, three quarters in length, wrapped around him like a shawl, concealing a shirt of pale yellowish colour and a black waistcoat. Covering his grey hair was a dull brown hat with a curved brim that sat loosely on his head.

He was a wise man and unlike the men of his age, Arthur was not one to take pleasure in "trivial social gatherings," as he called them, or "talking about the humdrums of daily life," or going on pub-crawls. These men, Arthur believed, were wallowing in the reminiscences of their heydays and their dreams of yesteryears, so instead, he preferred spending his evenings by the riverbank, thoughtfully reading and observing, and Dwayne started to do the same, spending some time, if he could afford to, in his company.

A year had passed. In a few months' time Dwayne would be 15, or entering adulthood as his, now trusted, friends called it. During that time, Dwayne and the boys developed between them a special rapport – a sort of mutual understanding of each other's attitudes and ways of behaving. And not only had the boys curbed their extravagant spending habits, but they also started showing Dwayne a great deal of deference and admiration, which he reciprocated appropriately.

"Brother, you are now one of us and nothing can harm you," they reassured him regularly.

"I'll be back in an hour, bro," said Ali as he headed for the door.

"Remember, no gambling," replied James, as if giving a warning to the younger member who was well addicted to gambling.

Dwayne marvelled at how mild in manner they had become over the year, in comparison to his perception of who they were when he first met them. They treated him like a younger brother, considering that he was much younger than they all were. They were bound to him and he quite liked that, though he was still suspicious of why exactly they had taken such an elevated fondness of him.

On one occasion, when the boys had gone off to some sort of concert in Liverpool, Dwayne made a remarkable discovery. It was late in the evening and Dwayne had just finished washing up the dishes left in the kitchen sink. Switching the light off, he traced his steps along the hallway leading to the living room and the other rooms. Straight in front of him, directly facing the kitchen, was a closet. He paused in his tracks for a moment. He had never seen that door unlocked, and he wondered what lay hidden in its dusty racks. His heart pounded as he advanced towards the locked closet. He was trespassing. No, he wasn't, he convinced himself – he was merely *looking*. He thought of his friends' reactions and the implications of his actions as he approached the closet and gripped the small handle. He pulled it towards him, but as he predicted, it was locked. Squatting down, he peeked through the tiny keyhole, but could see nothing apart from the dimness. Disheartened that he made no discovery, he walked back to the living room and reclined on the large sofa near the fireplace. It was a rather chilly night, so Dwayne pulled himself a bit closer to the fire and placed his feet on the extensive hearthrug, and upon doing so, a heavy dull sound resonated from underneath it. It seemed as if it was hollow beneath the rug. Curiosity got hold of him, and he cautiously lifted the rug and tapped the floor – the door to the cellar – several times to reassure himself that it was indeed hollow. He broke the lock with little effort and swung the door open. Darkness seeped from it. A wooden staircase descended from the entrance to a cemented floor, encrusted with dust that covered its entire surface, just as froth sits on top of steamed milk.

Dwayne descended the first few steps carefully. On his right, just below the fireplace, was a bulb, but the switch for it was nowhere to be seen in the darkness. Since he was alone in the home, Dwayne was hesitant about going down. He could even feel his fingers throbbing rhythmically, due to tension, and several rapid and successive pulses of fright ran down his spine. After running his hands along the walls near him, Dwayne found the switch and illuminated the cellar. Four large wooden crates were positioned side by side, and there were several other crates on top of them. The light exposed them as they sat, huddled, still and dead in the dark as an enemy waiting in ambush would. Beside the crates were numerous black plastic garbage bags lying around. In the far right corner of the room, also beside some crates, were small canisters and various bigger containers. These were filled with liquids and everyday household detergents, like thick bleach and kitchen cleaners, in large quantities. Dwayne was slightly perplexed. He hadn't the slightest idea as to what use these things had. He went over to the craters and carefully opened one of them. It was filled to the brim with black powder, but Dwayne couldn't recognise it. He opened the crate next to the one he opened earlier, and it contained the same substance … and then the next one … and the next … until he uncovered all of the crates. Bewildered, Dwayne stood in the middle of the cellar, trying desperately to make sense of what he had just seen. His mind frantically searched in all directions, beseeching the remotest areas of his brain to come up with an answer, but to no avail.

His head swirled. An excruciating headache started to develop, and Dwayne thought it reasonable to leave the cellar and curl up by the fireplace upstairs for some warmth. The cellar was extremely cold and he started to feel the muscles in his toes tightening. He had just placed his left foot on the first step when he noticed a brightly coloured book lying underneath the staircase. He picked it up and a sudden gush of fear and panic inundated him. *Where did this come from?* he thought, as he gulped down some saliva to quench an unknown thirst that had arose without warning … or was it the fear? His eyes were fixed on the book as he flipped its pages, one after the other, skimming through the endless words, illustrations and photographic images. In panic, Dwayne dropped the book and staggered up the stairs. On emerging from the cellar, he bumped into a large figure that almost pushed him back into the cellar. He looked up and there he was, standing face to face with James.

"I, I … t-thought you went t-to Liverpool?" he stuttered.

"I guess he's ready, brother," said Ali, the youngest of the bunch, standing behind the bulky James. He was three years Dwayne's senior.

"Ready for what?" Dwayne shot back. These guys were up to something and he didn't want to be part of it.

"Sit down, brother," said James pleasantly. He was calm and composed, which always made it difficult for Dwayne to figure him out. It was hard to understand a man whose emotions you never saw, whose face, always as blank as paper, revealed nothing. He had a phlegmatic attitude that was quite difficult to fathom, and Dwayne somewhat feared him. James gave a fleeting look to his comrades, and they went away.

"You remind me of my younger brother, Dwayne," he said as he reclined on the sofa nearest to the fireplace, extending his hands out to the burning logs. "That night when I saw you at the alleyway, alone, I remembered him. You look like him a bit, and that's why I didn't want you to end up like him."

"End up like him?" asked Dwayne.

"He was stabbed in Deptford by some Ghetto Boys. They stabbed him right in front of my eyes, man." A sudden stream of sorrow, followed by an air of melancholy, surrounded the warm room as he narrated the tale of his brother's death.

"You're still young, Dwayne, but don't worry. As long as you are with me, I won't let anything happen to you, you hear? This is your house!"

"Thank you," Dwayne replied softly, nodding. Such reassurance was what he needed. "And what is all that stuff down there?"

"Don't worry about it … it's to destroy the infidel governments."

"And what have they done to you?" Dwayne shot back without regard for any consequences. Dwayne had learnt about Islam from his neighbour Ahmed at his former Oldman Street the previous year. During Ramadan, Dwayne would fast with Ahmed and his family. And when it was time to break the fast, he would do so at their house. In spending whatever spare time he could with his neighbours, he developed an enthusiasm for the religion, finding, spiritually, some solace in it. That was after the London Bombings last year.

"They are the infidels, brother. They are killings our brothers and sisters in Palestine, massacring them without mercy in Iraq, torturing them everywhere they see them. Why should we be held back? Besides, we will be going to the Promised Land. Heaven, my brother, Heaven! Think about it, brother, we are going to be martyrs," he replied, as his eyes ignited with fury and delight at the same time. This subject made his emotions clearly known.

"So that's why you've picked me up from the street that night, yeah? That's why you looked after me all this time, so I could be part of your group?"

Dwayne was starting to put things together, and all the pieces fit like a jigsaw puzzle. *No wonder they sold their large Plasma TV and Radio equipment*, he thought to himself, *and stopped going clubbing.* He also remembered Ali once telling James, "Gambling is forbidden, bro," but never paid much attention to it at the time. So this was what it was all about.

"No, Dwayne. I picked you up from that cold pavement because I wanted you to have a better life. I know what it is like to live on the streets; I have been sleeping rough for three years, man, and I know how it feels. But now, that life is over. Now I want to bring peace and justice to the world."

Despite having slight fears, Dwayne believed him. However, in the back of his head, something troubled him greatly.

"You will kill some people in order to bring peace and justice to the world?"

"Come with us, brother. We will protect you and make sure you go to the Promised Land."

"I am not coming with you to kill people."

Dwayne's eyes shot at James in astonishment. He had to do something to stop these badly informed youths from committing grave mistakes and ruining the lives of many, but how and where does one start? Not only that, how does one get away from all of them? He couldn't think properly. Thick dark clouds spiralled in his head. They were probably the dark clouds Arthur had told him about – dark clouds that were "hindering" him from seeing past them. How could killing people bring peace? He did not understand.

"I won't let you kill innocent people."

"Go ahead and tell the police then. After all this time, Dwayne, that's what I get, yeah? I loved you, man, like my own brother. And now you wanna snitch on me?"

With that, James walked out of the room.

"Oh, God," Dwayne said with a soft sigh, his eyes still wide. He sat on the creamy sofa and stared into the fireplace. He needed to talk to someone – *oh, where is the old man?* Who was it that said a teacher was someone who knew something about everything and everything about something?

Arthur sat on his usual bench, holding a copy of the *Daily Telegraph* in his hands, when Dwayne came rushing towards him.

"Oh! How pleased I am to see you, Dwayne!" exclaimed Arthur. "For long you have been my sole companion and protégé, and your absence has but made my heart long for you. Tell me, how have you been, my son?"

"I am in a lot of mess, and I can't think of what to do. My whole life is messed up and I can't do anything to stop it."

"You are mature enough now, Dwayne, to make decisions for yourself, and now that both your mind and body have significantly developed, you'll soon, at full tilt, enter the world of adults, son. On your escapade, you will discover a new world of cruel nature. A world where injustice prevails and justice is long forgotten, a world where the insane outnumber the sane, where nations go to war at the beckoning of a finger; a world where the rich implore the poor, where the rich amass wealth and the poor descend into the bottomless pits of poverty. You have now come to face the realities of this world, Dwayne, and so you must!"

"But I can't, Arthur, without risking my life and that of my brothers!"

Brothers? Did he just call them brothers?

"My dear Dwayne, the heart of a person always seeks for and travels in the path it has always known – the path that brought it joy and contentment all along. There is richness, bliss, and a great deal of tranquillity in that path and, by the abundance of such desirable qualities, it promises much more. On its walls are buttresses to prevent unnecessary anxieties and concerns and torments of a harsh world. It is your only realm of independence and choice, where everything is pristine and pure. Here are neither restrictions nor limits, and your scope is as far as the eye can catch, and your thoughts are inexhaustibly transcendent. Where the normal rhythm of life oscillates between your monotonous daily schedules and inconveniences, here you may fail to remember them and explore the expanse of your salubrious surroundings. Like a raft without anchor or direction, gently floating upon the vast blue ocean, you can delve into your depths, wave upon wave, trying to perceive, in your autonomous existence, things imperceptible to you in the humdrum of daily life. It is in this serenity and self-possession that you lose virginity of your inhibitions and become yourself without pose or pretence. It is in that secluded environment that you look into the deepest recesses of your soul and question yourself: what is it that I want in life and where do I want to go from here? Then you will have all the answers that you crave."

Dwayne thought about the words of Arthur for a few moments to get their full meaning. He did not want to betray James and divulge the actions of his friends to Arthur or anyone, and at the same time, he wanted no part in it. As the night slowly crept in, he departed, keeping Arthur's words firmly in his mind.

That night he laid in his bed, squirming uncomfortably, his head throbbing with worry and fear. How would he decide on what to do? If the heart of a person travels in the path it has always known, then his heart has only known one path, but on that path, there was no joy or contentment, just uncertainty. "A loaf and lodging is all the luxury one needs in life," Arthur once told him. For a loaf, he could work for whatever he could find, but what about lodging? What would he do? Then an idea came to him, followed by a frown. He hated his life and wished for some sort of divine intervention. God! Why did he ever choose to go with them that first night! Then he remembered his aunt.

At the crack of dawn, the next morning, Dwayne packed his bag and left the house. His rucksack was the only thing that had stayed with him for as long as he could remember. His mother had bought it for him. He stayed at his favourite place, by the Thames Riverbank, all day and when the cheerful clouds had scattered and the sun had started its plunge down the horizon, Dwayne prepared his bed. His rucksack by his side, he sat against the wall of the same dark alleyway where he slept a year ago, hands clutching his knees, and slowly started to spread a towel on the cold floor. He watched as the flickering started in the dim, grey sky, and the shimmer of the bright lights along the riverbank illuminated the darkness like beacons, until they all gradually began to diminish, eventually losing their glow.

AYAN

Ayan reluctantly slumped down in her seat, adjacent to the window, submerged with anxiety. She certainly wasn't ready for this – not this early at least. She wasn't much of a traditionalist and didn't care much for the precedent Somali customs of ancient times. She was different. Different in terms of her intrinsically western customs and the new set of standards she adopted thereby. The closest she had been to Somalia ever since she emigrated from it twenty years ago, at the tender age of five, was by means of her television screen's constant depiction of chaos, bloodshed and destruction. During her time, the city would have been flourishing with flowers of every shade and colour; whereas jovial faces of young children smiling like spring buds would have marched the streets with hope and reassurance. Now all she witnessed was an ever-escalating violence, and the carcasses of dead bodies lying in puddles of blood that decorated the streets made her stomach churn. So why was she on this damn plane to Somalia now?

It was then that she remembered her mother and siblings from whom she was separated by the raging war, and her nervousness, for a split second or so, receded to the back of her brain. Her big bulgy brown eyes lit with enthusiasm as soon as she entertained such a thought and the anticipation of exploring what life would be like in those parts of the world, and being re-united with her family, gave her a vicarious thrill. The other part of her, by conjuring up images of havoc and destruction, made her feel reluctant to make this trip, parading her cosy apartment, in the heart of Greenwich, in front of her. However, it was the overwhelming desire she had for a mother's love, along with siblings, that determined her to go, overpowering any other setbacks and silent lingering doubts. She had not seen her mother for over twenty years and was devoid of her affection and care. And now she needed her more than ever!

The short hand of the clock struck 10. The seat belt sign came on, but Ayan had already tightened hers around her. Aeroplanes still agitated her during take off, though she had flown many a time. An uncomfortable twinge of fear grasped her every time she occupied an aeroplane seat, leaving her clutching its armrests firmly. It was no different today as well. With great effort, she reached for her leather handbag, which rested between her feet, and rummaged through it. After a short moment, she drew out her hand with her pink iPod, turned it on, and pushed the play button to release the voice of Bryan Adams. *"Look into my eyes, you'll see, what you mean to me…"* it started, and with this tuneful music lessening her fears, she was slightly relieved and closed her eyes. The lines on her forehead straightened as her worries faded into the background of the soothing music. She wasn't even aware of the Cabin Crew retreating to their designated places. A few moments later, the plane took off.

It was four in the afternoon in Bosaso, and the sun was still intensely oppressive. From her window, Ayan could see that the plane had landed on a coarse runway, between mountains, scattered with gravel and stone. A small brick house with a single large window and a tin roof occupied the centre of the airport. This was Immigration and Customs. Along its borders, the window was reinforced with a shield of iron mounted on it. Within a distance of a hundred paces stood another building; a larger house built in the same way as the former. "Bosaso Airport" was marked vaguely in faint colours of blue and white on a large white board on top of the building. Ayan assumed that the colours represented the Somali flag, but she didn't pay further attention to it.

The moment the plane came to a halt, a portly figure of a man in a steward's uniform – a white shirt, black trousers and bow tie – quickly appeared from nowhere and unbolted the door. It seemed rather odd that there was no announcement or anything of that sort. *There was none before we flew off either,* she thought, recalling her memories; but that was soon forgotten when she decided to alight the flight of stairs. A wave of baking heat greeted her, and her lungs seemed unable to inhale the boiling air. She was short of breath and the quick agonizing gasps of hot air scalded her throat, making her feel as if she was drowning. Huffing and puffing, she glanced ahead into the bright sunshine, her eyes squinting and her body trying to adjust to the severe conditions. With great struggle, she managed to balance her stilettos on the wobbly staircase and set foot on land. It was precisely 4:30pm, and she was officially in Bosaso, Somalia.

Outside the tiny brick house stood a chair and a table with a few pieces of paper and stamps on it. A dark bespectacled man silently occupied the chair and stamped the documents of the arriving people without once looking up at them. Behind him were three gun-wielding men in army uniforms, demanding attention insistently and loudly instructing travellers to get in line. One after the other, the travellers got their passports stamped and the queue shortened. When Ayan approached the table and presented her documents, the bespectacled man stopped what he was doing and pushed his thick glasses down the bridge of his nose. He looked up at her, then inspected her from bottom to top, his gaze ascending slowly. She felt uncomfortable and avoided his eyes. Looking ahead of her, she caught sight of the soldiers hungrily leering at her too. *But why?* She looked down at herself. She wasn't naked, but the piercing gazes of almost all the bystanders made her feel exposed. She felt disgusted. Later, she realised it was the jeans. *Why hadn't anyone warned her of the stigma that these jeans carried?* She was the spectacle for the day and by the visible sneers, hers was an unimpressive performance. She focused her eyes on her surroundings and tried to contemplate on what the future of her stay might hold in store for her in this godforsaken place, careful to keep all her thoughts modest. She observed that a barbed wire bordered the stretch of the airport, leaving just adequate room for the entrance of vehicles. Why hadn't her uncle come to pick her up? Standing in the scorching sun was unbearable, and not a single shelter or waiting area was in sight to hide from the heat. Uncontrollable trickles of sweat appeared on her forehead. She hated sweating profusely; she took out a pack of paper handkerchiefs from her handbag, wiping her face repeatedly.

A few minutes later, a white Land Cruiser, covered in dust, pulled in through the metal gates of the enclosure. Almost immediately, a long-limbed man stepped out and, with measured steps, looked around his surroundings in a calm and unruffled manner. Ayan caught sight of his actions and moved forward a bit to make her presence felt, to which he responded by beckoning her with a nod. As she got close, he locked her in a stifling embrace and, after a few moments, let go. She heaved a much-needed sigh of relief, and quickly jumped in the front seat and fastened her seat belt. This prompted him to turn his head slightly, for a reason she didn't know. He revved the engine and rapidly sped off, sending pebbles flying in mid-air.

A rough road rapidly rolled in front of them. The car bounced up and down at great speeds. Her uncle did not say much. From time to time, he gave her a fleeting look and then gazed directly through the windscreen. Ayan squirmed in her seat. The heat made her feel uncomfortable and, annoyed by the silence of her uncle, she initiated a conversation.

"How's mom and the family doing?" she inquired, and quickly bit her lip for asking such a silly question. She should know how her family was doing – she ought to.

"Fine," answered her uncle, still steadily gazing through the car's windshield.

There was silence. The roughness of the road and the heat, which she had temporarily forgotten, started to gnaw at her again. A few moments later, the road smoothened as they entered the city. Rows of concrete houses with beautifully decorated balconies occupied both sides of the road. In some houses the gates were of bright colours of red and green. Farther down the road, an assortment of huts with tin roofs sat adjacent to one another, as if huddling for warmth. Ayan's eyes carefully followed the buildings, analysing the area and observed its people – her people. She was deep in her observations when she heard her uncle ask, "Enjoyed your trip?" in a dull voice, without any passion or appeal.

"It was alright, Uncle. I thought it would crash any minute. It was very unstable," she replied.

"Hmm," he grunted without looking at her.

Ayan was in disbelief. *Why ask a question, when you don't want an answer?* she thought to herself.

Finally, to her relief, the car came to a halt. "Huruuse Hotel" said the large sign, which hung from the first-floor balcony of the four-storey building. She assumed that it was probably the tallest building in town. Her uncle stepped out immediately, as he did at the airport, and brought down her luggage. Stepping out of the car, Ayan went round to fetch her luggage. She crouched down to pick her bag up when a hand touched her on the shoulder. She looked up and saw her uncle standing tall. The sun had darkened his face and his black eyes sunk deep within it. With a caring stroke, he pushed the protruding strands of hair from her damp forehead and peeled the bits of tissue stuck to it. He then rested his hands on her shoulders. After gently placing a kiss on her forehead, he picked up her bags and moved toward the hotel.

She was alive once again. That affectionate kiss resuscitated her enthusiasm and hopes. She entered the hotel's tiny single bedroom and, kissing her uncle goodbye, took an obligatory shower, opened the windows and lay on her bed. Soon she was in deep slumber.

The following morning Ayan woke up early and started to prepare for her journey to her mother's home. Having packed, she stood at the balcony of her four-storey Hotel apartment and gazed out intently into the city, waiting for her designated driver. From her vantage point, she saw the clear blue ocean shimmer and reflect the cloudless sky. A gentle morning breeze fanned her long, jet black, hair and caressed her face, softly soothing her. She closed her eyes and inhaled the clean air in huge quantities, carefully drawing in each breath as if it were her last. Amidst the air wafted the strong smell of the sea, and Ayan was sure she tasted traces of salt at the back of her tongue. For once, she started to admire the expanse of the land and sea surrounding her. She looked down and observed people going about their usual business. A restaurant just below her hotel commanded her attention. She observed as a young girl, whose shiny bronze skin glared in the early sun, served tea and breakfast to a group of gentlemen sitting on plastic chairs set outside the restaurant. The gentlemen were engaged in a conversation when another man greeted them, washed his hands from a container and joined them in the food. A few moments later, a young boy approached the gentlemen with a bucket in one hand and shoe polish in the other, offering his services, which they politely declined. The boy smiled and went on approaching passer-bys, eventually finding a customer. Ayan at once admired the simplicity of life that they enjoyed. Tranquillity descended upon her, engulfing her altogether. Contrary to what she had in mind, combined with the miserable images that made the news, Ayan stood motionless and envisaged herself living in this environment – in peace. It seemed quite paradoxical, but she had created that image in her mind.

A loud telephone ring restored her from her dream. It was her driver. Quickly she dragged her bags down the stairs and stacked them in the car. Then off they went.

A few moments of driving and some sharp turns saw her in the middle of Bosaso. A long stretch of road – the only tarmac road she saw – dissected the city in two. Originating from the port, as her driver informed her, the road linked Somalia's northern and southern cities together, ending up in Mogadishu. They passed by the Hospital, a thousand and one restaurants, countless hawkers by the roadside, Lorries heading out and entering the city, people, goats, sheep, soldiers, more hotels ... and finally silence. No commotion-filled, busy and eventful street was to be heard – just the noise of rubber eating away the tarmac. Dry land occupied either sides of the road as far as her eye caught. Further ahead, great mountains towered above the levelled ground. The enormity of such mountains loomed over the vast barren earth and formed a pleasing sight.

The long stretch of road led them past the villages of Laag, Karin, Laasa Dawaco, and Ceel Doofaar, upon which the driver came off the road and took a narrow path formed by the tyre tracks of cars and by constant usage. They followed that rough route through countless villages and, after a gruelling five-hour journey, set foot in the village of Booxaaro. It wasn't exactly a village, for a village consisted of at least a few houses, a community and some neighbours. Here, the vast land was, for the most part, unoccupied, except for a house that conspicuously took up its rightful place in the middle of nowhere. There were hardly any trees either, apart from the few dry trunks that stood like solitary soldiers assigned to keep watch and guard their surroundings. Beside the hut, a thick fence formed a large ring. Inside it, animal dung had plastered the earth, covering the thin layer of soil, but there were no animals present.

From the hut emerged a child no more than five years of age, his eyes dazzled with enthusiasm upon seeing the approaching car. Behind him, a tall woman walked briskly, shouting at the boy to stop.

"Ka joog Waryaa!" she screamed, and the boy stopped.

She was about 45 years of age, and it was obvious by the finely-tuned features, though baked by the sun into a dark chocolaty complexion, she must have been without comparison in beauty during her glory days. As the car approached, Ayan's heart hammered heavily in her chest, threatening to crack her ribcage open. She even thought she heard its pulsating beats. A reservoir of tears gathered at the brim of her eyes, ready to gush out at the very mention of the word "hooyo" – mother! She had become devoid of sensitivity and emotion. For twenty long years she had longed to hear those words of affection and love, and it was now she was the closest. The car hadn't even come fully to a halt when she pushed the door open, jumped out, flung her arms around her expectant mother and silently sobbed tears of delight, relief and excitement.

It was a common custom among the nomadic settlers that if they owned a large number of camels and one of them went missing, they would risk life and limb, utilising everything in their disposal to get it back, and until they found it, would spend night after night in discomfort, swimming in seas of worry. Ayan's mother was no different, and despite having the other seven of her offspring, the return of her missing daughter brought joy to her eyes. And though she, being the sturdy woman she was known to be, strongly repressed it, a thin layer of water formed in her eyes and then dropped like brightly glittering pearls, slowly sliding down the slopes of her face. Gradually Ayan's heart came to rest, and the thudding was replaced by a wave of comfort. The warmth of her mother's embrace disposed of her restlessness, evaporating her concerns and worries into thin air and putting her troubled heart to rest. Everything else seemed insignificant now; her mind was for the first time completely free! That was where she wanted to be and that was how she wanted to feel. In that very instant her life changed and, without regard for what perils and tribulations lay ahead, Ayan decided that this is where she wanted to spend the rest of her life – under the shelter of her mother's hut. The rest of her siblings were away, dispersed into the immense terrain, and so Ayan grabbed her youngest brother, gently pulling him toward her as they went inside the hut, still clinging on to her mother.

... To be continued from here

Be Strong Brother

Of life's boundless bounties and offerings
Too comes entwined many great a suffering
With hardships and many troubles to overcome
And pains to which many a weak might succumb

When in your chest your heart heavily pounds
And you are startled by the very subtle sounds
Be strong, my dear brother, be strong
And lure your organ to mellifluous a song

Though your lips are parched and insides churn
Implore not a soul and to them ever turn
For such traits defile the dignity of a man
Inviting derision and disgrace to last a lifespan

What with your hands you gradually sow
Will soon take form and start to grow
And the earth sets forth its plenteous yield
Enveloping your dignity in a protective shield

But when misfortune upon you smiles
And life all its burden upon you piles
Bear the patience to make it through
For only from that springs strength anew

Show, in the face of adversity, resilience
And be in the times of distress steadfast
Abstain from crying to anyone in grievance
Sullen be not and fly thy flag at half-mast

Be wary of the feelings nourished by hate
Lest they come to haunt you at a later date
And since hate begets nothing but hate
It gives birth to defects and a doleful state

May you find contentment in your heart and refuge
From the tremulous seas and the tempests ahead
From the glowering clouds and the hurricanes so huge
From the doubts and difficulties that you so much dread

From the spiteful souls and the sins they conceal
From the covetous and the contents of their cauldron
From the glittery gifts of this world, how so unreal
From moments of grief and the agony that goes on

And what do we learn from grief but gallantry?
For when in the dismal depths of despair
Like the procession of a loved one to a cemetery
One often returns with courage and a prayer

Ephemeral pleasures

Though soothing a sight the sunsets may be
And the ocean's silence – a solace for the sore sight
Slumberous, still, and wading birds waddle with delight
As calm waves kiss the sandy shores and leave their trail
But soon that turns to turmoil, come the tempest overnight

Though magnificent the moon may be
Dazzling In the distant enchanted land
A visual feast, so hypnotic and grand
And the Nightingale its mesmeric melody sings
But soon all fades once the sun takes command

Though delighted once a person may be
Possessed by the gaiety that fills his air
Without much dread and less for care
But when it comes the time to grieve
Soon all his efforts turn into despair

Though now willowy, at the peak of your prime
And many marvel at your graceful manoeuvre
And pompous gait and gloat, too busy to discover
That covertly it creeps and calamity will befall
Alas! The infamy of age and all will be over

Though steadily fleeting with time,
Your profound beauty remains
As pure as white, as heaven ordains
Like a Lilly that gently floats
On top the placid pond it reigns

Though in its full blossom and ripeness
Your sight is but a pleasure to the eye
Even to the larks that twitter in the sky

But like an ocean of bluebells in May
Soon that fades come the month of July

So bask yourself in its rays while it lasts
And live and laugh to your life's delight
For even one kissed by the summer's light
Though becomes merry for a time prescribed
Surely awaits seasons of mist and wintery a night

Go ahead my dear and rejoice while you can
And fragrant wreaths and garlands make
For even the flowers that opened at daybreak
Too become dreary and dull at the dawn of dusk
As darkness from their petals all glory does shake

Tears of happiness

Have you ever cried tears of happiness
That on the cheeks do gently flow
Upon the sight of a special someone
Whom your life and joy duly depend
But separated by need and necessity

Like a caged bird that is set free
Do your wings now feel the breeze
As they flap and flounder and finally fly
Chanting and chirruping for all years of solitude
Soaring and diving to your heart's delight

Like a blind man with his sight regained
Does your heart convulse in rapturous merriment
Has the greenness of the grass blinded you
Or the splendour of that flowing stream
Whose roar you've always heard but never saw

Had they been translated into words
These tears would tell rivers of tales
And flow into streams of endless sight
Meandering through the barren ground
Swallowing a pain inexpressible in words

The burden tears unveil in the silence of the night
Through them finds this weeping heart solace
A strange paradox mother, yet the silent tears roll
And it is your thoughts o' noble queen that help it
And envelop this feeble body in a cloak of peace

And when you sleep and put your mind to rest
Know that every waking day a son thinks of you
And for every single thought a tear would fall
For when you are apart and separated by fate
A mother's love manifests itself most profound

It Pains Me

Oh how this pains me mother I can't express
This enduring absence from your eyes
And though dearly dissembled, this distress
Is easily discerned despite my disguise

Oh how the music of your voice and soft hums
The melody that once was a solace and soothed me
Now reverberates on these cold and empty eardrums
Yet still echoes songs that fill the heart with tuneful glee

And when you start to grow old and grey
The beauty and wisdom that you possess
Which never weaken with age or wither away
Will continue to guide me into a peaceful bliss

In my humble heart there is a special place
Reserved only for a mother's love to fill
For her love no living soul could replace
Even if despised who would love you still?

A love so strong that never fades or falters
A mother provides with nothing left to spare
How magnanimous, for her sympathy never alters
As she continues to nurse with such benevolent care

No words of praise could express it, however lofty
A love that defies every obstacle, however daunting
No tears could drain or diminish it, however plenty
No love could equal or surpass it, however unrelenting

Oh how this pains me mother I can't express
This perpetual absence from your eyes
And though dearly dissembled, this distress
Is easily discerned despite my disguise

The Lonely star!

O' you solitary star, that in the distance weeps
Whose tears like surging streams do flow
Or like drenching rain come down in heaps
Why have you my dear lost your glow?
What ails you my star

Oh this void, this sorrow and what I conceal
What a cruel world this place can be
And though even the aching heart can heal
The wounds of loneliness won't set me free
And it is this that ails me my dear!

Though on the outside you are bright my star,
But with the darkness dribbling from your surface
And shadows akin to smog and soot carving a mar
Your brawn and brilliance have dwindled but a trace
Pray tell, what ails you my star

I hear that I am a sordid sight
But with no one to share my plight
And no might to even put up a fight
let me wallow in self-pity this night
And it is this I feel right my dear!

O' you lonely star that in the distance weeps
Before this disfiguring darkness eclipses your face
Brighten up and dispose of the dejection that creeps
Lest you lose what's left of your glory and grace
And this I fear for you my star

Tribute to my Aunt – *March 2006*

There will be a time
When we'll meet again
Yes, there will be a time ...
Now that you're gone, as is ordained
May your soul rest in peace and your abode be the grandest
Where birds sit and sing you their sweet melodies all day long
Where the herds of trees lower the fruits on their branches
May you wake to a place
A fragrant land glistering with dew
And serene landscapes of greenery to soothe your sight
With tulips, daffodils and roses everywhere you tread
As you hear the waterfalls roar in the distant woods
And the soft breeze caresses your skin and titillates your ears
Where cool springs and streams of milk and honey do flow -
May your eternal home be surrounded by
May your nights be cosy and warm, free of all worry and stress
as you surrender to ultimate tranquility
May your soul rest in peace!

May your soul rest in peace!
as you surrender to ultimate tranquility
May your nights be cosy and warm, free of all worry and stress
May your eternal home be surrounded by
Where cool springs and streams of milk and honey do flow -
And the soft breeze caresses your skin and titillates your ears
As you hear the waterfalls roar in the distant woods
With tulips, daffodils and roses everywhere you tread
and serene landscapes of green to soothe your sight
A fragrant land glistering with dew
May you wake to a place
Where the herds of trees lower the fruits on their branches
Where birds sit and sing you their sweet melodies all day long

May your soul rest in peace and your abode be the grandest
Now that you're gone, as is ordained
Yes, there will be a time …
When we'll meet again
There will be a time!

Haybad waxaad ku leedahay dhulkaaga Hooyo!

(dignity you have, only in your Motherland)

But where do I belong?
Where do I call home?

Where can I walk with pride
With my head really up high
With no guards by my either side
Rest under a tree and look to the sky

Where can I live permanently
Where can I leave a mark?
Without having to transfer frequently
And comfortably inhabit and work

Where can I sleep soundly in my hut
Knowing that I am safe and secure
Without having to be vigilant and alert
And awake with my heart guiltless and pure

Where can I watch my kids grow
Watch 'em as they play on the streets
Without fear of attack and brawl
And congregate loved ones for perfect feats

Where can I walk around freely
Without being asked my tribe
And intentionally robbed greedily
Or imprisoned and enslaved for bribe

Where can I live individually
Without having to carry a gun
Live the rest of my life peacefully
And ultimately quiet down and have fun

Where do I belong
Where I craved for so long
Where I really must call home
Where?

WE ARE NOT INVISIBLE

Adam Dirir

Adam Dirir : Founder of Somali Eye Media
   Have you ever thought that you could accomplish your dreams after shear graft and determination? Adam Dirir has done just that. In July 2003, along Brighton beach, Adam thought of his brainchild and decided to embark on setting up a Media Organisation for his community.
   Adam was born in Somalia and there weren't many role models while Adam was growing up, but he didn't let that stop him from achieving his goals. Adam has travelled to many countries and has picked up a number of different languages along the way, but it has always been his passion to give back to the community and aid others that has been his driving force.
   Adam Dirir has set up Somali Eye Media from scratch, which produces Somali Eye Magazine *and runs the* Somali Voice Radio *in Tower Hamlets.* He is a dedicated writer and community activist. Much of Adam's work reflects his commitment in encouraging the Somali community to aspire and develop their strengths. He is a well known figure amongst all communities in Tower Hamlets and often interviews many leading people from the area. Above all Adam would like to write more in depth about the lives of Somali people both in Britain and abroad in the future.

What does it feel like to be British Somali? That is a question that I am often asked. I say to you all that deep down in my heart, I feel invisible because that is the way many Somalis feel. We, as a community, have been here in Britain longer than most people think; we are not an emerging community but an invisible one that others have chosen not to understand. But that does not mean I want others to make my identity for me.

During the Second World War, some 375,000 men and women from African countries served in the Allied forces. They took part in campaigns in the Middle East, North Africa and East Africa, Italy and the Far East. Men of the 81st and 82nd West African Divisions served with great distinction against the Japanese in Burma. The 81st was composed of units from the Gambia, Nigeria, Sierra Leone and the Gold Coast (now Ghana), while the 82nd comprised further reinforcements from Nigeria and the Gold Coast. Both Divisions formed part of the RWAFF (Royal West African Frontier Force). The King's African Rifles was composed of units from Kenya, Uganda, Nyasaland (now Malawi), Somaliland/Somalia and Tanganyika (now Tanzania). The KAR fought in Somalia and Abyssinia against the Italians, in Madagascar against the Vichy French, and in Burma against the Japanese. These Africans – considered by some of their own British officers to have been undervalued and underused as front-line troops by the British commanders – proved extremely hardy and tenacious in several battles, both as combatant soldiers and as medical staff, carriers and other auxiliary participants. Every veteran has his or her own war, and each is custodian of a unique story and memories.

There are the physical hardships that can't be mitigated by advanced technology. There is the noise, the confusion, the chaos, and the uncertainty of battle, no matter how great the odds are in your favour. And there is the longing for peace, for the calm of a day without bullets or bombs. They are charged with the mission of undoing the damage of war. The process starts with corpsmen, working along the front lines to treat the wounded, risking their own lives in the process. It continues in the field hospitals and then further away from the battlefield, in the convalescent facilities, staffed by tireless and resilient doctors and nurses. No job in any hospital is preparation enough for the relentless task of dealing with the wounded and dying of war. The outcome of any armed conflict holds not just the promise of peace but also dark, terrible revelations, questions of justice over the vanquished, and, for far too many, the confronting of personal loss.

"Every soldier learns in time that war is a lonely business," wrote Matthew Ridgway, one of America's great generals, who served in World War II and Korea. In the face of Ridgway's accurate observation is any soldier's sense that, in battle, the man on your right or the man on your left could be the man who saves your life.

Farah Ibrahim Abdillahi, as a Somali veteran, came to understand that, as lonely a business as war can be, the camaraderie planted in basic training and nurtured through the hardships of the battlefield is a powerful weapon against fear. This is his story:

"I was 15 when I was first called for duty; 06/06/1942. At that time, I lived in Burao, Somaliland. I robustly trained for 3 months non-stop in Madheera, situated in the middle of Berbera and Hargeisa. I was young, enthusiastic and willing to learn. I felt buoyant when I was awarded my first medal one month later. I was trained with men who were in the army for up to 14 years. I felt really good about myself. We were taken to Baabule in Ethiopia for more training and after that, we moved on to Kenya where we met other East African Soldiers. We were told to unite with them. This was fine with us although we didn't take too well to their 'uniform.' As Muslim men, we are not supposed to uncover our legs, and these soldiers wore very short trousers, which looked like something I would wear as underwear!

As Somalis, we consider ourselves tall and handsome, and those short trousers would never do us justice. In Kenya we were served 'Ogali,' the local traditional dish, which didn't do anything for my taste buds. Oh! How I missed my traditional camel meat and fresh milk. We were part of The King's African Rifles, enjoining five different East African countries, better known as KAR. I fought in the war against Japan in Burma. We won that war and famously the Japanese confessed that they were overtaken and beaten by tall and thin men. The last soldier to shoot his gun in that war was a Somali Soldier. After the war, we all returned to our countries. I went back to Somaliland holding my head up high. The trials and tribulations of war were finally over. I was proud of what I had accomplished for myself and my fellow Somalis people. I am also proud of all my medals awarded to me by King George VI. The memories are still vivid in my mind like it was yesterday. There were seven of us; Mr Adan Caydiid, Mr Mohammed Ismacil, Mr Muse Cawale, Mr Cawale Joraan, Mr Askar Oday, Mr Hirsi Faarax and myself. Mr Adan Caydiid was awarded the MM (Military Medal) for bravery.

The ceremony was held in London and I can still remember how I felt when the King shook my hand. It was a great privilege. I also took part in the Falkland war in 1982. I was in the navy then and took part in a war that was completely different from the Second World War. You don't see your enemies anymore. We were stationed miles away in the sea and all we did was bombard Argentinean posts. There were many sacrifices made by Somalis for this country in both World Wars and since. I am proud to be Somali and British. I am now a proud father and grandfather. I always instil in the young ones courage and pride in everything they do. There is nothing wrong to be part of this country, and do not allow anyone to make you outsiders; we are now part of the fabric of this country."

Somali Eye Magazine October 2006

I was very lucky to meet up with Mohammed Farah, the European Championship Silver Medalist. We met up for a coffee and I was able to put forward a few questions to him about his recent success at the Championships. I started by asking him how it all began. He had a huge grin on his face, which remained there throughout the whole interview.

"I have always loved sports and I can still remember my PE teacher (Alan Wilkinson) at school encouraging me to take up running seriously as I had the potential. I was only 11 then. Alan took me to a running club but I didn't like it initially. I wanted to be a footballer as all young boys do and I had no idea I could run so far. I didn't want to return to the club, but Alan bribed me, as he didn't want my talent to go to waste.

He told me that I could play football for half an hour before training began with my friends at the club. This was really encouraging. Looking back now, this was one of the best things Alan could have done for me, even though it was a little cheeky! My training was going really well and, before long, I was running with kids that were much older than me. I was really disappointed when I came 9th in my first professional race. Only the first eight runners were going to be put forward for England. I hated seeing the other kids with their England shirts. This anger pushed me to train even harder, and I was determined to get an England shirt of my own and be put forward for the National Team. I came first the following year."

I asked Mohammed if that feeling was similar to winning the Silver Medal. He told me: "It was very similar, but winning the Silver Medal was just that slightest bit sweeter as I also broke the record to become the second fastest man in England ever." Mohammed's grin disappeared for a while as he told me about his disappointment at coming so close to first.

"I was really close to grabbing the Gold Medal; it was only a matter of seconds, but I'm still really happy with my Silver Medal, and at last I have something to show for all my hard work," he said, with his trademark grin returning.

Finally, I asked Mohammed how he felt holding up the English Flag when he won his Medal.

"I was really proud," he told me. "Even though I was born in Somalia, I am a British Somali now. I have been in this country since I was a child and have been educated here; I feel very much British as well as Somali."

Somali Eye Magazine July 2006 3

Now, what about me? It all started when I fled from the Civil War in 1988 at a very early age. My family and I went to Diridhaba, Ethiopia, and stayed there for two years. Ten of my family members, including myself, my aunty and cousins, immigrated to London, UK, in October 1990. Coming to the UK was a new experience; the weather was so wet and freezing cold that even my internal organs were shivering! In the first two months, whenever I saw students walking in the area I lived, I would stop them, point at their uniforms and bags, and ask: 'You, School, Where?' When the kids replied back, I could not understand a word they were saying but instead, I used to look at their body language and see where they pointed. Then I would go in that very direction and look for a building, which I thought was a school. Anyway, I managed to find secondary schooling with the help of my relatives. I started attending Holloway Secondary School in North London from year nine. One of the funniest things that happened to me was when my elders or those who arrived in the UK before me used to tell me that I should watch out for the kids in the school, or they would bully me. Here is an example of me taking their advice without being careful. A student (in the same class as I was) came up to me and said 'Give me five' (meaning high five in this case) ...

I instantly remembered the warning I had been given, so I got up and punched the other kid. The student just stood there with complete shock! I suddenly realised that I made a mistake. I did not know what to say. Even a simple 'sorry' was impossible as I could not speak English at all. As I had never seen white kids my age before, I used to get confused over who was who, constantly mixing up their names.

I was able to finish secondary school with the help of Allah (SWT) and by taking after school classes, along with ESOL. After completing high school, I went on to study at

City & Islington Sixth Form Centre in Holloway, North London. I began by taking three A levels in Chemistry, Biology and Math. After six months of studying my A levels, I was told by my tutor to start studying BTEC National Diploma instead, and the reason I was given for this move was that my English was poor. When I look back,

I think of that advice as discouraging. However, I moved on and completed 'BTEC National Diploma in Science.' I then went onto higher education and obtained the degree of Bachelor of Science (BSc) in Pharmaceutical Chemistry at Queen Mary and Westfield (QMW), University of London. Throughout the years of my student life, I worked at McDonalds Restaurant as part of the weekend staff. The money I used to earn during this period was for my expenses and for sending remittance back home using 'Xawaalad' (the Somali money transfer system).

After graduation in June 2000, I started working for Boots the Chemist as a Healthcare assistant from Monday to Friday. I stayed with McDonalds Restaurant until I became a Shift Manager during the weekends. I wanted to carry on further education and receive a postgraduate degree. Somehow I had to come up with the fees, whether it was by taking out a loan, sponsorship or working full-time and paying it myself. Well, I did it the hard way, working seven days a week for three straight months. The money I saved up from the two jobs over the course of three months was enough to pay off the fees required for a Masters Degree. In the year 2001, I was the only person to complete a Master of Science (MSc).

I am not the only one who has persisted in my dreams and efforts, nor am I the only one wanting to bring about change. Cabdulahi Maxamoud is the first elected official of Somali descent in Britain. He is proud to be in this position and, rather than just be satisfied with his achievement, he is always hard at work, encouraging others like him to aim for high positions. He is a true role model to the Somali population in, not only his Ward, but also in the wider community in Britain.

It was the year 2002 when he became an elected official, a 'councillor,' for the local government in the inner city area of Southwark in London. This area includes one of the largest public housing estates in Europe. London is a city with large diverse populations and in its section of Southwark, there is a larger share of this diversity. This includes a relatively large population of people of Somali origin. However, the Councillor is keen to point out that he was elected on a ticket of the Labour Party and that he did not receive any substantial backing from Somalis as such. Councillor Cabdulahi feels very strongly about the local Somali community. He encourages them to feel at home, to get involved in the local community around them. He feels that the Somalis are becoming, more and more, a part of the UK.

Councillor Cabdulahi worked very hard to fix local problems, such as the shortage of home and the lack of employment. He feels very comfortable with representing a diverse community in his Ward.

"It is not hard to explain why I enjoy this," says Councillor Cabdulahi. "I find it easy, and I enjoy being with a diverse group of people. I enjoy it very much. I think because when my grandfather settled in Kenya, he was living in a country with a large number of languages and cultures. And he had come to appreciate living with this large diversity."

His grandfather had come from Somaliland to fight with the British in the Somali Camel Corp during the 2nd World War in East Africa.

He had achieved a tremendous amount in the short time he had been in London and is holding a very important post in the local government.

He is making a difference in the lives of those in his Ward by speaking up for them and assisting them in accessing service in the Council. He is also proof of that which a Somali person can achieve with hard work and drive.

There is a Somali proverb, which says "aqoon la'aani waa iftiin la'aan," meaning, "without knowledge there is no light." But knowledge used is also power, as there are those who use knowledge to hurt and damage. Articles such as "The Suburbia's Little Somalia ... ", which appeared as a main feature in the Daily Mail on 12th January, 1999, portrayed Somalis as ' ... violent, drug-takers, cheats, bogus asylum seekers and criminals ... '

This is how the national media portrays the Somali community to the wider society. Since this is what makes great news, it can be easily digested without question. How easy it is to assassinate our character. Our achievements are invisible because, for some reason, they do not make great news. The Somali community faces deep-rooted prejudice, which is related to racism and Islamophobia. But we are here, and we have a positive contribution to make to British Society. I know I am here to stay; I am part of the diverse British society that makes Britain, Great Britain.

The Noble Savage

Abdi Bahdon

PROFILE: *Abdi Bahdon, also known as Book of Rhymes*

Abdi Bahdon, also known as Book of Rhymes, is a talented poet, lyrist and actor. This young African-born performer is only 18 years old and has already accomplished a great deal. He starred in a short movie called 'Mash Up,' as well as the television program, 'The Bill.' However, in a recent interview for Sheeko magazine, the young actor stated that his real passion was lyrics and music. "When you are an actor, you are just playing a role, but in music you are portraying yourself. The person you are and the person you want to be or become."

Abdi's lyrics in his songs are very personal, and evoke anger and sorrow from the listener. He manages to draw from his life experiences – experiences that seem to be something straight out of a tragic drama, rather than real life.

Born in war-torn Somalia, Abdi was subjected to appalling violence. During the Civil War in Somalia, Abdi was badly injured as a result of a car explosion, which left his right arm paralysed and his ribs broken. After several attempts to rectify the damage, the doctors in Somalia removed nerves from the back of his legs and placed them in his arm, yet there was no improvement. Abdi was now left with even more scars, not only from the flying dauber and fire, but from the post operational scars. He lost his family and friends as he fled the continent with a group of refugees and was later abandoned. From such a tough experience, many would crumble under the emotional stress and head toward a life of crime. However, these experiences have made Abdi stronger. In an interview, Abdi said, "I have been through too much just to give up on life. I want everyone to *know how hard life is back home in Somali. I don't want to be in that sort of pain anymore, so I try my hardest to succeed for a better life."*

Abdi is not only succeeding in acting and music but he is also achieving amazing progress academically. He arrived in London at the age of ten not speak any English and now at the age of eighteen he has manage to achieve nine A-C grades at GCSE level and is now currently studying A levels in Sociology, Physiology and English. His work record is excellent with all tutors citing his hard work and sheer determination to excel as his key strengths. Abdi takes full advantage of the College facilities and regularly attends workshops and additional learning support groups.

Abdi started his acting career in Langdon Park School, where he studied drama. He found it exciting, enthralled by the fact that he could "be someone else for a day." He started searching for roles in local productions, eventually working with places like Half Moon Theatre in Limehouse.

With the taste of acting on his tongue, Abdi then auditioned for a part in a short film, which he later got. The film follows low-life London teen Robert as he enters a pigsty of a flat, telling his twitchy friend (played by Abdi Bahdon) a story about a day he spent with another friend Marlon trying to find 'hash' (marawana). At one point, Robert is beaten senseless by a gang of girls, but they eventually find the drugs and all seems well until Robert realises he has been injured in the brawl. At this point, reality floods in on him. This short 10-minute film addresses the aggressive, violent London youth culture and contains a hidden anti-drug message. This is why Abdi decided to take part in the film. "I did it because the message behind it was so important. I feel that London teens are wasting their lives and the opportunities they have on meaningless experiences."

This short film brought about the opportunity for Abdi to be part of an O^2 advertisement, which became a nation-wide billboard campaign that worked to attract new customers to the O^2 mobile phone network. The film also brought about the role in the television series 'The Bill,' in which he played Adem Yusuf (episode 1 in 2007), a young Somali boy trying to gain citizenship in the UK in order to support his family back home. Abdi said that this story had a real element of truth to it. "The youngsters in this country that are by themselves have the burden put on them to provide for their families back home. To them, we are seen as adults, but in this country, we are told that we are still children.'

Clearly a man of many talents, 18-year old Abdi also writes his own music and produces it himself. With songs like 'Dear Father,' which was a track dedicated to his father who passed away in the Civil War, there is intense emotion and feeling pouring from the notes. He also made a track called 'Coconut-Noses,' which is a humorous song that addresses the problem he faces everyday, in which people stare at his disfigurement. Abdi says music is "... a way I can release my anger. It allows me to deal with my inner most feelings and hurt."

No matter whether its music, films or television shows, Abdi Bahdon (stage name 'Book of Rhymes') is destined to achieve big things.

"I am 'Book of Rhymes.' I am like an open book full of musical rhymes. To me, this is an original angle, as if I'm looking into a different world. I believe that there was never a life as hard as mine. I had no family, no love, no money, and no direction in life. I only followed the true voice, my voice. The voice inside me. That's the voice that has the story to tell, therefore I will tell it exactly as I experienced it. I believe my work is like art, and it comes to me like an inspiration. The best way to understand what I'm writing about is to understand my mind which is the force that drives my inspirations. I cannot truly comprehend the way I feel about my past which is why I believe my poetry is unique in its nature. It is constantly shaping the person I am and at times it leaves me in uttermost uncertainty. I believe my future is always changing but never do I feel "That's Who I Don't Want To Be!!"

Interview with Abdi Bahdon himself

The Dead Tree

I saw a dead tree.
I Took a good Look at his roots … they were dying slowly.
I Looked at his dead dry leaves … they were falling slowly.
Then I realise.
That there is only one place U can find this Dead Tree … .
"In The Cemetery".
Then I looked at my self in the mirror
And I saw my reflection
I saw the Dead Tree Again.
That Dead Tree represented Me! and My People Back Home!

"We need to establish Peace in our hearts, before we establish Peace in the streets of Somali, because Peace, love and freedom comes from within." Lets pray that Peace will come!

Poverty is the name!

Close your eyes
And picture this
Poor Hungry lonely children are crying.
Rich kids smiling.
Angry mothers cursing!
Afraid of being outlasting!
I am sleeping,
And I see the hopeless not breathing!
I Am screaming!
"Give the hopeless
A helping hand"
We need to understand
That we are falling!
I Am slipping!
I Am losing!
I see too many kids dying,
Because they are Starving!
We all share this name
And we all share this pain!
"Poverty" is the name.
We are all prisoners of this poverty,
But We need to break free
To survive.
Poverty is like living in a world without windows
And the rich see this life as simple.
We need justice
I Decline
To live with this name
But always Poverty will be our name!

Father!

My first child your name on it
My second child Ur fathers name on it
And if it's a baby girl your mums name on it
Father u have a place in my heart
The right side … but not the left side
Father that's how much I miss you
And how much I love you
I wish I could trade my soul
So u can come back home
And u can comfort this lonely soul
Daddy … Most girls think I am romantic but I think I am dramatic
Here we go again this is just me being ironic.
Father I know u passed away 18 years ago
But until today I am still crying tears
I know you were a soldier
And am proud to be the soldier's son
But I swear to GOD … until the day I die
I will always miss U
Talk to me daddy!
Your last born is "Missing U"
I Miss U (May Allah Bless Your Soul)

Welcome To My World!

Welcome To My World!
Dear Reader!
I look at my self in the mirror
And I see my reflection
I see this boy looking back at me
Begging for affection
And I see too much information
Then I ask me too many questions ... Daddy what did I do?
I think mummy gave birth to a black curse So what could be worse?
I never deserved to become disabled for life Daddy I got 22 scars And I don't even know how I survived Am only 18 ... ?
And am still crying like a baby boy
I cry because I don't see any peace
Only what I see
Is a hate and grief, in this society?
In my community ... they say we live in equal society ... but are we?
That's a rhetorical question
So come-on ... and answer for me!
People we need to face the fact that we don't live in an equal world So welcome to my world!
Let me begin ...
When we were born
We were warriors,
We lived in a peaceful place
Called heaven
In Africa.
But! ...
Suddenly they came
They took us away
And they turned us into slaves.
We were in chains,
We cried and begged

For our freedom.
We were caged like hungry black dogs,
They put us in human carriers
Across the Atlantic
It felt like a mission to hell
No one was well,
Because our soul was lost in the wind.
It was beyond human thinking.
They sold our soul
In the devil's market
"Slave for sell"
But the price was economical.
We cooked for them
We cleaned for them
And in return our women got raped!.
We cried out loudly for mercy,
We ran like fugitives
But our feet were cut off
Because we were running for our freedom
Like "Kunta-Kinte".
We never gave up running, until we became free.
I think the past will never die out in our minds.
The past will always be a total human exodus and eradication
Obliteration!
And extermination!.
Excuse me dear Reader
But today!
I cried …
I cry because I don't see any peace
Only what I see
Is hate and grief,
In this society.
In my community …
They say "we live in equal society" … but are we?
That's a rhetorical question!

So come-on ... and answer it for me!
People we need to face the fact that we don't live in equal world!
So ... close your eyes and picture this ...
Can you see my world now!?

Another slavery nightmare!

I saw a ghost from hell!
How can I tell?
If I was well
He told me about the Voodoo spell
He had over my people
I said my people are hopeless and helpless
And I have nothing, expect a dream of freedom
I told him ... I can't think of anything good
Coz my heart is purple
And I am Clueless
I told him I can't spell
But I can spell the word "Equality"
He said ...
U r a slave of this society
I said ... what about the Morality
He was speechless
He looked at me ... with two dreadful eyes
And he put his white hands over my head
And he left a scar
Suddenly I opened my eyes
And I realise
It wasn't a reality
It was a dream
Another slavery nightmare!

The Anxious Mind

There is no justice in my mind
So when … I look at my self in the mirror
I see my reflection
I see this boy looking back at me
Begging for affection
And I see too much information!
Then I ask my self too many questions … father what did I do?
I think mummy gave a birth to a black curse
So what could be worse?
I see my destiny when I dream and it is full of darkness
Full of hate, grief, pity and bad spirit,
Fear and paranoia … got the best of me
Every step I take calculated for me … an early ending,
Am falling down
Like a falling star
The person … who I see in the mirror
Is not me
Is my malevolence past! And the dead corpse … whom I have cursed!
And If I get the opportunity
I will probably kill you first
For reading these black cures!!!
What I see is me!

"P"

I swear this wasn't my plan
Why pain and stress
Are always on my chest
I can't rest
Why do you want me to confess?
And feed you the best
Before the rest
I can't cry
I can't smile
And I don't look up to the sky anymore.
My soft heart
Is turning to a black stone
I never asked for this
To be the centre of attention
They wanted information
Too many personal questions
Coming from different sides
Like shooting bolts
I tell them to leave me alone in "P"
But!
They want more
They are hungry for more
They want to hear my past life stories
My nightmares!
I tell them one story
Just the intro
But they want to hear the next episode
Then!
They say with an outlandish voice
"We feel so sorry for you"
Overall
Has no matter of fact
I don't need your shooting roses

Plus
Read my lips
I don't need your f***ing sympathy.
    Leave me alone in "P"

Do they care!

I saw my spirit standing above me
Stirring at me with two lonely eyes
Asking me why did I wish, the wish of death?
I thought of death too many times
In my sleep …. But that was only a dream
That doesn't mean I wanna die
I just wanna cry
So I can realise my pain
If there is a way
When there is a fear and paranoia
There is no love
I don't trust any body
Not even my own lady
Is probably true what they say
I live the life of a loner
But is a bit hard to grow up without a father, and a mother, and a brother, and a sister
And I wonder if I was a milliner. Would they cry 4 me when I die?
Since the day I was born
They said
I was an impertinent child!
I was wild
Naughty by nature
Like a noble savage
But!
That was part of me growing up
Part of my childhood.
I believe we all dream
When we sleep
But I dream about
The name they gave me
"Black Rose Was The Name!"

Dear reader
"This name can speak for him self"

I was raced up in the lonely dark
There was no mercy for me
I believe I am different from other roses
Am a black rose still living in the dark
Question: why?
I am sure you read this black book
What can u see?
Nothing but pain

Now
The black rose is breathing his last breath
He is dying
But the name
Still standing
But Do They Care?

Letter to The Horn

Laila Ali Egge

My name is Laila Ali Egge. I was born in Somalia shortly before the outbreak of the war. After the political turmoil in the region turned into a full-scale civil war, my parents fled with me and my brother into neighbouring Kenya, and eventually into the United Kingdom. My mother and father both had family members who had come as economic migrants to the UK prior to the war; as a result, we were able to settle and adjust to our new lives relatively well.

I started my education in England from primary school, and I am now in my third year of University, studying International Relations and Development Studies. Coming to the UK from such an early age meant that I had no recollections of Somalia as a country before the war; yet, as a child, I was oddly proud of being a Somali, possibly because I had been told that Somali women, next to Ethiopian women, were among the most beautiful women in Africa. When I refused to sit still as my mother often combed the knots in my hair, she would tell me stories of these beautiful ladies and their elaborate beauty rituals, which included bathing in milk and honey to soften their skin. Not only that, but she would always point out that they combed their hair. That said, she had my full wide-eyed attention.

As such, I felt very smug about my ethnicity: who needed Snow White with her pale skin when I had a permanent golden tan? Princess Rapunzel can keep her timid and obedient straw-coloured hair. I felt blessed with my mass of unruly black curls.

I went through primary school with this confidence, but as I was growing up, I began to encounter challenges to this perception of my ethnicity. Every time Somalia was mentioned on the news, images of carnage, emaciated children, and men running around with

Kalashnikovs were all I saw. I was shocked, ashamed and dismayed by the images. My mother had always explained to us that the situation at home was precarious, but never in detail. Never so starkly.

It was during this time that I first understood that I was a child of war. I was a refugee. The word sounded ugly and hard. Asylum seeker. I tried that for sound. I didn't like the tone of that either, but being a practical child, I decided it sounded softer and was marginally better than the word refugee. I was an asylum seeker. I remember cringing with embarrassment in secondary school when the movie Black Hawk Down was showing in cinemas. I was an angst-ridden teenager going through puberty – the last thing I needed was to defend a whole nation to my fellow and equally angst-ridden classmates. I protested in vain to the cruel taunts by students, who said that the people on the screen, referred to by the American soldiers as the 'skinnies,' bore very little resemblance to Somali people, but that was just small detail. In secondary school, nobody ever lets small details get in the way of their fun.

For this, I resented Hollywood (which might explain why I have a penchant for foreign films). I felt as if they were washing my dirty linen in public. Was it not enough that my country was engaged in a long and drawn-out national suicide? Did the whole world really have to press its nose up against it and witness it as well? Come to think of it, maybe the title, 'Whole Country Down,' would have been an apt title for the movie.

I also resented the Somali people. Why had they allowed themselves to exist in a stateless state for so long? How many people had to die? How many children had to be born in strange lands before change was insisted upon?

It was during this period of 'depression' that I began to research everything about Somalia; it was as if I needed to arm myself with facts about my fatherland. My great uncle was a great help. He had left Somalia before the outbreak of the Civil War, coming to the UK as a sea man to work in the British sea ports in the 1960s. I spent hours listening to him tell me how life was in Somalia before he left. His account of our land differed completely to what I saw on BBC and CNN news, and I was greatly moved. I had lost my faith when it came to my country, and he gave it back to me. It was through him that I discovered that the great British Explorer Richard Burton in his book, *First Footsteps in East Africa*, had dubbed Somalia a nation of poets.

"The country teems with 'poets, poetasters': every man has his recognized position in literature as accurately defined as though he had been reviewed in a century of magazines – the fine ear of this people causing them to take the greatest pleasure in harmonious sounds and poetical expressions, whereas a false quantity or a prosaic phrase excite their violent indignation."

This was great news. It meant that we had other talents, apart from killing each other. Why had no one bothered to mention this about Somalia? More importantly, it raised some questions. How many other possible great things that could have emerged out of Somalia have been strangled by war? How many geniuses have been forced to abandon their books and pick up a weapon?

The following prose is written in the form of a letter that I imagined my uncle would have written to his native land. I know from his accounts that upon arriving in the UK, he had terrible homesickness. His aim in coming to Britain was to accumulate enough capital and then go back; he always maintained that it was only the outbreak of the war that prevented him from returning home.

Letter to the Horn

Dear Beloved,

It has been a long time since my eyes beheld your wonders. Many a year has passed since that fateful November night when my comrades and I crept upon a dingy boat and left your shores. Beloved, with age my memories have faded, but no, not completely. For it would be a lie to say that I do not remember the smell of fresh goat's milk in the early morn, or the sounds of the decorated women ululating for the gold-adorned youthful bride. The smell of mild musk and the bold vibrant colours of the silky dircaas[*5] worn by ladies of esteem still linger in my mind. Tell me; do the Somali women still inspire even the most illiterate of fools to compose a couplet on the street?

Beloved, what of your mountains and of your coastlines? What of Hargeysa, Mogadishu, and Bosaso, and what of my people? Hot blooded and proud.

Tell me of the sandy beaches of Berbera – do the foamy waves of the sea still caress and flirt with the shore as before? Does the call of the muezzin, calm, crystal and clear still herald the break of dawn and rouse the faithful from their slumber? Do the unruly youngsters still grumble from his admonition that 'verily, prayer is better than sleep?'

Tell me; is the marketplace still the loudest place of all? Do those witty traders still sell precious stones next to cumin spice from old India? Ah, what of the children ... do they still run around with bare feet, carefree and wild? Let me know of the nomads who roamed the countryside, stubbornly never setting roots but dependably followed their herds: do they still posses the poetry tongue?

O, how I miss it all, like a lover missing his love. O, how I yearn for the dusty heat and the loud bustling noises! It now seems to me that those noises announced that we are indeed living, that we were breathing and our blood was young.

---

5   Dircaas, long colourful dresses worn by Somali women

Where I am now is a cold, cold, place and my old bones ache from the chill. We subsist in isolated units and silence is cherished. The modern life creates a modern strife where neighbours no longer have the need to exchange neighbourly fires.* [6]

In the old sayings of the wise, it was often said that 'those that eat alone, choke alone.'

I looked out my window the other day and saw an ambulance parked outside. A few onlookers, strapped in their jackets, were huddled close together as a stretcher was carried by. I found out later that his name was George, a WW2 veteran whose heart had failed in the night. It took a week before anyone realised the gentleman had passed.

The land replied:

My Son,

Much has changed since you sailed. Indeed, it was not long after you left that mercy fled and kindness was shackled. The youth of whom you speak of – anger enshrouds their hearts, consuming their minds; they are wedded to the guns. Their irrational thoughts spur on irrational acts. Adding to woes, more woes with their acts.

The air is dry, and my back cracks from the heat of the punishing sun. The heavens in their anger withhold their blessings; instead of rain, I have blood to quench my thirst.

I am forced to entomb many who fell short of their grey hairs, and the wise fools no longer hold council under my trees[7]. The camels no longer give abundant milk, the women carrying water on their heads no longer sing. Instead, they strike at their chests in grief and lament; dishevelled mothers burying their seeds scream 'Put away you arms!'

Their cries fall on deaf and mutinous ears. Death has made a permanent home here.

---

6 The practice of exchanging hot coals to start a cooking fire between two neighbors
7 Old Somali men used to sit underneath the trees to discuss affairs of the community

Letter to the People

My people, until you unite, you will always be weak. The wise will attest that our differences we can overcome. Do we not share a belief in the One? In earlier times, before the Europeans came, did we not live as one?

The past is done. Blood cannot wash out blood. An eye for an eye will make the whole land blind. Will you allow the Horn to be the place that time forgot? While you are out there masquerading in your antiquated arms, the world has moved on. Look around you ... do you not see death? Do you not see brutality? Do you not see the misery that your ignorance and pride has wrought?

My people, rise up and cast out the toxic warlords; cast them out. Their wars are void of liberty, void of glory. They deprive a mother of a child, a wife of a husband, a son of a father. They are holding you in darkness, holding you in bondage; in your own land, you're held hostage.

Did you not free yourselves from European colonialism? Did you not shed your blood to free yourselves from American imperialism? How is it then that you cannot free yourselves from being enslaved to Russian arms?

My people, it is better to light a candle than to curse the dark. Throughout history, freedom and peace have never been bestowed as benevolent gifts: Rise up and act! None, but ourselves, can free our land. None but ourselves can free our people from guns.

www.ingramcontent.com/pod-product-compliance
Ingram Content Group UK Ltd.
Pitfield, Milton Keynes, MK11 3LW, UK
UKHW021304180426
11947UKWH00015B/1001